S0-BKG-963

CCH
CONTEMPORARY COMMUNITY HEALTH SERIES

Autistic Children

AUTISTIC CHILDREN
A Working Diary

Florence Milnes Kozak

UNIVERSITY OF PITTSBURGH PRESS

Published by the University of Pittsburgh Press, Pittsburgh, Pa., 15260

Feffer and Simons, Inc., London
Manufactured in the United States of America

Library of Congress Cataloging-in-Publication Data

Kozak, Florence Ann Milnes, 1948–
Autistic children.

(Contemporary community health series)
Bibliography: p. 171
1. Autistic children—Case studies. 2. Kozak, Florence Ann Milnes, 1948—Diaries. 3. Psychologists—United States—Diaries. I. Title. II. Series.
[DNLM: 1. Autism—in infancy & childhood—personal narratives. WM 203.5 K88a]
RJ506.A9K685 1986 618.92'8982'09 86-7034
ISBN 0-8229-3539-2
ISBN 0-8229-5383-8 (pbk.)

for my son, Ian Alexander
for Karen & Todd

—for all you have taught me,
all we have shared

Contents

Introduction

This book had its beginnings more than ten years ago, when I was a graduate student pursuing a master's degree in clinical psychology. My goal was rather a vague one, but it included working with disturbed children. The trouble with the degree program, which struck me very early in the first semester, was that we never got to see, let alone work with, any real people. Of course, the rationale was that until we had some academic theory under our belts, we would not know what to do, anyway. Although this reasoning made sense to me, the courses being offered were so poor and uninspiring that I soon found work as a volunteer in a special education center, squeezing in time three mornings a week between my classes.

I was assigned to a classroom of emotionally disturbed children, and the teacher gave me one child to work with as I wished. This four-year-old, Karen, had not been diagnosed at all, except informally, in whispers, as "psychotic." She was quite classically autistic: she toe-walked, hand-flapped; she had little spontaneous speech, made little or no eye contact. I was surprised that no one else, professional or not, had seen she was autistic, but as a first-year graduate student I kept my mouth shut. The only name I associated with autism at the time was Bruno Bettelheim, so I dug his books out of the library and read him to help me with Karen. For many years after Leo Kanner had first identified autism in the 1940s, it was considered an emotional illness, a failure of maternal bonding. And this is the way I approached Karen's problem in our one-on-one, unsupervised, unquestioned sessions.

Part 1 of this book, then, is the diary I kept of these sessions. I kept it because I wanted to remember as much as I could about our time together, and because I hoped it might help me put some order into these new and often confusing experiences. After some time it also occurred to me that such material might be helpful to others who were planning to work with similar children; it could, at the least, help to answer the question, "What is it *really* like to work with these kids?"

Implicit within the material of part 1 is my "rescue fantasy," naive but sustaining (at least for a while)—my belief that Karen was a normal, indeed, extremely sensitive and intelligent child hidden in an autistic cloak which my love and attention could strip off. My time with her ended with my pregnancy; soon thereafter, her family moved to another state, where she was correctly diagnosed and placed in an autistic classroom. She is now a teenager. Several years ago her mother sent me her photograph; she is still beautiful, but to me the keenness of her face seems irretrievably dulled.

My degree and my son Ian arrived within a few weeks of each other, and I spent the next four years being a full-time mother. The relationship with

Karen was still very much with me and could not help but influence my style of mothering. For example, I spoke or sang to him almost incessantly, nursed on demand, and in my efforts to make sure he would have enough stimulation, even took a toy with me to the hospital in case childbirth and its aftermath proved boring. (It didn't. Ian is now eleven years old; he talks or sings constantly.)

During this time, I also read as much as I could about autism, discovering that parents of autistic children had rebelled against the guilt caused by Bettelheim's hypothesis and had fought successfully against it. Largely through their efforts, autism is now classified as a developmental disability, along with cerebral palsy, mental retardation, and epilepsy. It is defined behaviorally, by a cluster of symptoms, and so is technically a syndrome, not a disease. These symptoms include the inability to form normal relationships with other people; the absence of speech, or its delayed and impaired development; the presence of abnormal or bizarre responses not only to people but also to physical objects, situations, bodily sensations. Many autistic children have repetitive patterns of activity, like flapping an object or shaking their fingers; these actions are called "stims," short for self-stimulating behaviors. Autistic children who are verbal usually have verbal stims; others' may range from the merely socially inappropriate to the self-abusive, even life-threatening.

Needless to say, I was forced to rethink all my experience with Karen. In my naive fumbling, I had helped a little, but not enough, because she was organically wrong somehow, miswired. I had misinterpreted what I had seen because of my preconceived, Bettelheimian bias. Indeed, I had gotten very angry when Karen's father even brought up the possibility of brain damage. That error caused me pain. The very thought of Karen continued to cause me pain, and I resolved to continue working with autistic children.

My chance to continue did come, and my journal of those experiences comprises the second section of this book. I was living in a large metropolitan area and answered a newspaper ad looking for staff members for a group home serving six autistic boys which was in the process of opening. I worked weekends in this home for over two years, often substituting during weekly shifts as well, as a behavioral technician. My job title indicates the difference in milieus; the boys, too, were very different from Karen. They were not given at all to sitting and flicking their fingers; they were extremely active physically, and aggressive tantrums were common. I was, of course, not given *carte blanche* as with Karen; I was a staff member and worked with the others to develop behavior programs for the boys.

Group homes are an increasingly popular alternative to institutionalization for many handicapped people. Their goal is to normalize the lives of these people as much as possible, to teach them functional living and social skills. I have tried, in this section, to impart the flavor of group-home life, which is undeniably bizarre and yet undeniably human and touching. However, for several reasons the story of the boys is not as compelling as that of Karen. The one-to-one intimacy she and I routinely shared is, for the most part, gone; also, there is less sense of growth and movement in the boys' personalities, which makes for less inspirational reading. This contrast is real, and is part of the reason I thought to put the two experiences side by side in book form. My time with Karen was special and rare; my time at the group home could be characterized as life in the "real world" of mental health work, where helping children loses some of its romantic aspects, but does pay the rent.

And as I had done with Karen before, in the group home I accepted the prevailing medical diagnosis—this time, that autism is a developmental disability. Now, with the benefit of double hindsight, I have come to be cynical about accepting either, or any, dogma as *the* truth. In the conclusion, I have tried briefly to evaluate my disparate experiences on my own terms and see what questions might fruitfully be raised on that basis.

For now, I would like simply to share some of my most intensely lived moments with some extraordinary children, in the hope that reading about them might be interesting and useful to others. My fondest wish is that some reader might be inspired to work with, and for, autistic children, or, better yet, that readers already in the field might be moved to more compassion. I really don't know how else you *can* react when you look up from your paperwork on the couch to see, on the table next to you, a naked prancing nine-year-old experimentally dousing his not very clean foot into your mug of cooling coffee!

I would like to thank my parents, Bruce and Lucile Milnes, for, minimally, securing my type-writer, and Larry Lewis for, minimally, moving my desk.

Autistic Children

I. Karen

Karen's records do not contain a formal diagnosis, because at the psychological testing session required for entrance into the special education program, she only screamed. In the classroom, she does not play at all with the other children; during the first few months, she mostly sat under a desk and screamed. Although she does not play yet or talk, except in isolated words and echolalic phrases, there is less screaming, and her teacher, Tonia, feels she is capable of making substantial progress.

Some other notes I remember from all that Tonia mentioned about Karen:

She loves to jump on the trampoline, both by herself and with an adult.

She loves music and singing. Tonia, for example, sings to her when it is time to go to the bathroom, and she responds well.

She must be taken to the toilet, and helped; otherwise, she soils herself, which is upsetting to her.

She loves to perseverate on the knobs and needle arm of the record player, and also on a toy cash register, which Tonia is sometimes forced to hide from her.

She loves to play in the swimming pool. Her class goes twice a week to use the university facilities. Now, however, ever since an attendant threw her in the pool twice and she sank to the bottom each time, she is fearful and cries.

Although sturdily built, Karen doesn't eat well. Tonia seems to think she subsists mostly on soda pop and doughnuts at home. She was bottle fed as a baby, and according to Tonia, never really graduated to solid foods. Her mother just kept putting all her foods into a bottle.

January 21

Tonia had told me Karen was a stocky girl, but I found her to be tiny, with fine black hair cropped close to her head, and delicate Chinese features. When I first saw her, she was sitting hidden in a corner, playing with her cash register, but she came to me willingly enough, with a little prodding from Tonia, walking on her tiptoes.

Before I arrived, she had been learning the names of some plastic fruits and vegetables, so I took the bag of them along with us for a start. She had said some fruit names for the first time that morning; apparently, after her long Christmas vacation at home, she is receptive and eager for some stimulation.

On the way to the large empty room we were to use, we stopped in at the bathroom. I took my turn at the toilet after Karen, and no sooner had I sat down than she took a step backward and fell down two stairs, banging her head into the door. I got to her as fast as I could, and with no hesitation she fell sobbing into my arms. We shared a good hard hug. While I was upset that she had hurt herself, I felt that the hug was a good sign.

We started working a bit with the fruit, but Karen had already tired of that activity and found my sneakers of much greater interest. As I watched her, I could see very little posturing that could be called bizarre—pained or awkward might be better descriptions—but she did make awful grimacing faces when displeased, and her communication for the most part consisted of wild sounds, not screams but low-pitched animal shouts. Her grimaces discouraged me, and I began to respond to them with bright beaming smiles. At first she was surprised, but then I began getting some return smiles, although only a few.

The hardest part of relating to Karen, I was quickly finding out, was first getting and then holding her attention. She allowed virtually no eye contact and she constantly perseverated on favored objects. Over and over she felt the textures of my shoelace and the metal eyelets, with a rhythmic flicking motion of her finger.

For a few minutes I got her to thread the shoelace in and out of the eyelets; she said "push" and seemed to understand the concept, so I tried to distinguish between "push" and "pull." However, she soon went back to flicking her fingernail on the shoelace. I was at a loss as to how to keep her attention. I felt as if she knew when I was trying to teach her something, and would immediately turn away.

I left her with my shoe and went to get a record player. When I returned, she hadn't moved an inch—only the finger, still flicking. She got very excited over the record player, which she knew well, turning all the buttons off and on. When the music came on, she sang along with some of the words, and we danced together, holding hands. At the appropriate times in the record, we clapped and marched and jumped. During the rocking part, I lay on the floor on my stomach and she lay crosswise on top of me, and we swayed back and forth. Mostly, however, we went round and round in circles. I got very dizzy, as Karen would not allow any change of direction. I assume she got dizzy, too, but she did not show it.

Soon Karen was needing more and more prodding before she would participate with me at all; finally she sat down in front of the record player and repeatedly moved the needle back to the beginning about every half minute. I sat down, out of her field of vision, to watch her. In addition to moving the needle, she loved to stare at the grooves in the record, and especially the paper-covered center as it whirled around and around. She watched so *very* intently; she reminded me of my cat.

Thus we sat for ten or fifteen minutes. Then, when Karen had turned the volume down very low (she never turned it up very high), I began, almost idly, to pick up the plastic toys and ask Karen what each was. "Corn," "apple," "orange," "banana," (pronounced *so* delicately, with short *a* sounds), "plum"—she knew them all. I added the lemon and then the potato. She seemed to like these sounds especially, and rolled them around in her mouth a while before letting them fall out.

Suddenly, we were all over the room with the fruit; the record player was forgotten. It was as if the respite in her private world had invigorated her, refreshed her so that now she could learn again. "Where is the banana?" "Can you bring me the apple, Karen?" "What is this?" "Po-ta-to!" Although she kept a tangerine in one hand and tended to drift off, twiddling the stem between two fingers, I was able to bring her back for much longer periods than previously by asking her to bring me a particular fruit.

When she finally did grow tired, she kicked the fruit or knocked it out of my hand, but usually the correct one. After she said "lunch" a few times, I realized she must be hungry and that this was a good time to end our session. Back in her classroom, I held out my hand to say good-bye, and she quickly, shyly, touched it for a moment. We had spent an hour and a half together.

I told Tonia what we had done and she was delighted, saying that Karen had never before been out of the classroom with someone for that long. Also, she had never before said "potato"! As I left, I could hear her loud shouting begin.

January 23

Not a very auspicious beginning today: as I walked in, Karen was sobbing. Somehow she had torn off a fingernail and the skin right off the top of the finger. I needed Tonia's help in getting her down to our room.

We spent the whole hour working on the alphabet. She can sing her ABC's in part, with help, and can discriminate some of the letters when I point to them in her Dr. Seuss book.

I had to come later in the morning today—10:30 instead of 9:30—because the class has started their swimming again. So lunchtime at 11:30 cut us short, while Karen was in a "perseverating period." On Monday there had been time for her to come out of it and do her best at the end, but not today. She did let me carry her all the way down to the basement to the lunchroom, where she immediately and accidentally knocked over her neighbor's milk. I had to say goodbye amidst a tumult.

There seemed to be much less of her private vocalizing today and fewer grimaces. Especially when saying a favorite letter (like *p*), her face would be very relaxed and beautiful. Her body posture seemed more relaxed, too, although perhaps I am merely getting accustomed to her awkward movements. I do not hesitate to touch her, but I never force or prolong a touch if she is out of contact at the moment and jerks away from me, which is what most often happens. Once she spontaneously came and leaned against my back for a few moments.

It is very frustrating when she does withdraw from me and perseverate; today she constantly flicked her finger on the book pages. During these moments she would not let me touch the book, or her, and sat with her back toward me. I had to slide along beside her, within her peripheral view only, and sing the ABC song loudly as I pointed to each letter. This method of getting her attention worked only occasionally.

I think I have taught her to identify a few pictures in the alphabet book, although perhaps she knew them already. It is impossible for me to know what she knows and does not say, or to know which words she is saying for the first time.

January 25

I have been reading Bettelheim and think I now better understand the importance to Karen of the times when she perseverates and ignores me. She is torn between the stimulation she so sorely needs and wants, and the fear she has of making this contact. Bettelheim feels that only with time and patience can a child like Karen overcome her fear, and she will have to do it in her own time, not mine nor anyone else's. To respect this, and not become discouraged or hurt, is my task.

January 28

This morning Karen was sitting slumped at a table, her back toward the door. She had been acting so depressed all morning Tonia feared she might be sick.

"Look who's here, Karen!"

Karen's eyes riveted on Tonia and remained there. I stepped into her field of vision. Immediately her eyes focused, and shone.

"Take–off–your–coat!"

She leaped at me and pulled off my jacket. A small tentative hand reached toward my face and was quickly rewarded with a kiss.

"Round–and–round–the–'berry–bush!"

Although the words "take off your coat" were often spoken to her, it was the first time she had spontaneously and meaningfully uttered them.

Tonia warned me that Karen's parents reported she was up to two "accidents" a day, and that she would need to go to the toilet shortly. However,

Karen resisted my efforts to get her into the bathroom, and her only loud grunts at me during our whole time were elicited by these efforts. Then, just before entering the lunchroom at our session's end, she popped into a stall as we passed through the large, open bathroom, and went all by herself! Add the fact that the bulk of her "perseveration time" was spent in examining her arm and picking off innumerable specks of an invisible something, and it occurs to me that perhaps Karen might be beginning to be aware of her body and her ability to control her functions.

Our session today started off jubilantly, with Karen repeating, one after another, all the words, songs, and phrases we had worked on last time. It was as if she were telling me, "See, I didn't forget. I remember us." I was surprised at how much eye contact she was allowing and how relaxed her face was. So we did a little work; she said a few new words, but her heart seemingly wasn't in learning new things today. Quicker than usual, it seemed, she retreated into her perseverative activity.

A group of women appeared in the doorway, looming large from our floor-level perspective. One pregnant woman, who loomed the largest and who was obviously the tour director, asked me if I were a speech therapist. I said no. She turned to the rest of the group and began, "Karen is . . ."

"A–B! C–D! E–F! G!" I sang out loud and clear, so Karen and I wouldn't have to hear what exactly it *was* that she was. They stared at us for a while and then left. I was glad to be able to stop singing, as it was embarrassing for me to have to sing in front of strangers. Karen had been picking at her arm the whole time, never looking up.

She began to fixate on the pencil sharpener in the corner of the room, her back to me. I lacked the energy to do any coaxing; I stood and watched her, tired and rather discouraged. Karen must have sensed how I was feeling, because she suddenly threw her caution to the winds. She ran toward me, smiling, arms extended. Without a pause, I caught her up: legs wound around my waist, arms clutched aroung my neck, head laid on my shoulder. I marched up and down, around and around our room, singing gently, pausing only to kiss her ear once in a while.

> *"Round and round the mulberry bush*
> *Round and round the mulberry bush*
> *Round and round the mulberry bush*
> *On a Monday morning!*
>
> *We can laugh and we can sing*
> *We can laugh and we can sing*
> *We can laugh and we can sing*
> *On a Monday morning!"*

She would lean back once in a while and look into my face, both of us smiling at each other. She also seemed to notice the lighting fixtures for the first time and often reached up toward the brightness.

I began to wonder how this session would end, because neither of us wanted to stop hugging each other. A little boy from Karen's class appeared to announce it was lunchtime, but Karen clutched at me even harder.

"Ba–by. Close–your–eyes."

So I closed my eyes and we made another pass around the room. Then she leaned backward from the waist until she was parallel to the floor, and said "swing." I had totally forgotten that I had swung her around a few times during my last visit, quickly and dubiously, because I didn't think she would like it. Now she was requesting a swing, and in such a precarious position, too. I held her as tight as I could and swung her around. A laugh of pure joy came out of her. I could not believe it. Karen had actually laughed!

She slid out of my arms and slipped her feet into her shoes. I asked if I could carry her downstairs, holding out my arms to her. She came.

January 30

Our session today started off in a subdued tone, in great contrast with Monday–no singing or dancing and very little response to the alphabet, although *p* did draw a laugh! She would not allow much eye contact, and I noticed she was restless, several times wandering out of the room, something she had not done before.

Tonia had given me a pencil to write down any new words Karen learned, but Karen took it from me and twiddled it so close to her face that I was afraid she would poke her eyes. Suddenly, in the midst of twiddling, she shouted at me, "Stay here! Stay here! Stay here!" and began to sob painfully. I took the pencil from her, meeting no resistance, and pulled her into my arms. We walked about the room. Her crying stopped, but at one point she leaned back, shouted at me again to "stay here!" and jabbed at my chin.

I carried her over to the light switch and said, "Turn on the light, Karen." She immediately looked for the switch but on the wrong side of the doorway. "No, it's over here, Karen." She turned her head, found the switch, flipped it, and looked up at the now glowing lights. This exchange was a very simple one, but most important: we had achieved our first real two-way, two-part communication.

She got down from my arms of her own accord. The rest of our session was spent mainly in body contact. As she sat twiddling pages of her alphabet book, I caressed her back, and then her head and chest, arms and legs. She let me do this for a long time before she moved away from my touch.

Her own body awareness continues to grow. She says "hand" frequently, and in a totally different tone of voice than usual–in wonderment, almost awe. After she says it, she looks at me strangely, as if for confirmation. I showed her my hand today, which she took in hers and examined very carefully, reminding me of a little monkey. Also, today she lifted up her shirt clear to her collarbone for both of us to view all that exposed flesh.

The words which seem to have most meaning for Karen she whispers. Today she repeated "ba–by," almost inaudibly, and also "tickle." I told her over and over she was a good and pretty baby, and she seemed to smile to herself. While caressing her back, I intermittently ran a tickling finger along the side of her neck. She responded, and seemed to enjoy it.

On our way to the lunchroom, she again used

the toilet by herself. Although she does not allow me to come into the stall with her, I spied on her and saw she even used toilet paper this time.

Lunch was a catastrophe. Karen pulled me down to sit by her, and I did not have the heart to leave. Aside from indicating I should open her thermos for her (eyes closed, she drank the entire contents in one gulp), we shared virtually no more contact. The small lunchroom was very noisy. Attendants milled around, telling particularly loud dissidents to shut up in no uncertain terms. Karen reverted almost completely to "autistic behavior," including loud shouting and a peculiarly vocalized breathing rhythm.

The specific goal of the attendants around our table was to get Karen to eat the meat in her sandwich, something I am told she has never done. She eats the bread and the meat is wrapped up to be taken back home. One attendant was quite forceful in telling each child what to eat, in what exact order, and she especially beleaguered Karen, at one point saying in an ominous tone, "*I'll* get Karen to eat her meat."

January 31

I ran into Tonia on the street today. She said Karen has been depressed since I have started coming to see her. She said Karen is attached to me, attached to someone for the first time in her life, and she is depressed when I am not there.

True?

February 1

I virtually snuck over to the Center today for an unscheduled visit, hoping that no one would realize that I was not in class where I was supposed to be.

I discovered that someone else will be working with Karen on Friday mornings for a while, and Tonia asked me if he could observe our session today. He is a student from the Special Ed department and will be working with Karen on her use of "expressive language." That choice of terms seems strange to me, since Karen's language is nothing if not highly expressive! For example, every time she looked at this heavy, deep-voiced stranger, she emitted loud grunts.

Our usual room was occupied, so we had to use a much larger one which had a stage at one end. Mike sat on the stage with a notebook and stopwatch, taking baseline data. Karen and I worked with the plastic fruits and vegetables and then her alphabet book. When she tired, she asked to be swung. "Swing!" Finally, she lapsed into a major perseverative period, carefully picking at each hair on her leg. For the life of me, she resembled a chimpanzee grooming herself, oblivious to whatever chaos might surround her.

Mike, meantime, had gotten down from the stage and had scooted over on the floor closer and closer until he was sitting with us.

"She tuned you right out, didn't she?"

"She had to, to protect herself and get refreshed. She's being hit with so much stimulation."

"That's why *you* think she does it, right?"

"That's what I think."

After a few minutes he left, figuring all the action was over. Slowly, Karen came back, this time to my body. First she gave me a few tentative shoves, then she wanted to be carried around and around the room, as is by now a usual procedure.

Today when I carried her past a window, I finally got her attention focused on the scene outside. Always before she had concentrated on the sill or a piece of paint peeling off the wall. She recognized the trees and repeated the word several times with delight.

We also spent some time in the trampoline room, jumping together. The mentally retarded class was also using the room. Karen related to them pretty well—at least, no grunting!

An Oriental woman came to observe, most likely another university student. She noticed Karen right away because of her Chinese features, and came up to us.

"What's his name?"

"Karen. She's a girl."

"Is she retarded?"

"No."

Karen only stared, silently.

A couple more items of note from today:

When twiddling the fruit, Karen sometimes held the apple or pear in one hand, and with the other made motions as if pulling something off the stem or perhaps the stem itself, and then twiddled this invisible part between her two fingers.

She gets such a kick out of the letter *p*. It finally occurs to me to connect it with "pee"!

She continues to show that the word "hand" has special significance for her. Also, she pulled up her shirt again to show her belly and chest to both Mike and me. I hope I showed sufficient appreciation!

February 4

Tonia told me that Karen did her best ever in swimming today; she trusted the instructor fully for the first time and did not cry at all. I hope that she is generalizing her trust in Tonia and me to others.

We had a quiet, undramatic session. As usual, her first words upon seeing me were "Ring 'round mulberry bush." This has become our theme song of sorts; we sing it at each session with all kinds of variations. Another tradition is that she tells me to take off my shoes as soon as we get in our room. After I have done so, she methodically removes both laces. This makes it hard for me to make a fast exit, as I am sure Karen is aware. She now spends less time twiddling with the laces than previously, although she still does it with a systematic persistence.

Grooming her legs took up a lot of our time. She did, however, look up at me once to say "*my* hand." I thought the addition of the pronoun very important; she connected her self and her body in this way for the first time, at least in my presence.

Once or twice she hurled a plastic orange across the room with great gusto and some laughter.

When I touch her and she does not want the contact, she says emphatically, "Yo! Yo!"

She continues to add to her repertoire of actions involved in going to the toilet. Today for the first time she pulled up her pants by herself. Always before, she had seemed unaware of her nakedness and hurtled toward the lunchroom au naturel.

February 6

Today was an exceptionally good session. I was the most relaxed I have ever been with Karen, and she responded to my increased ease by increasing her own. She was dressed in a blue smock-type blouse with her arms entirely bare, and her hair seemed to have been trimmed even closer to her head. She looked fresh and clean and very beautifully Chinese.

The word "big" appears on every page of the Dr. Seuss alphabet book, and I have been spelling it over and over to Karen, today more often than before. She can spell it out easily enough, but never puts it together, out loud at least. Today, however, I said, "Where's *big*, Karen? Show me *big*." And she pointed to it!

Karen likes to grab the book away from me and start twiddling with the pages, her back toward me. Usually I let her alone for the most part, trying to recapture her attention only vocally. For some reason I felt playful today and would not stand for this rebuff. I repeatedly put my arms around her small hunched body and hugged her, saying I liked this and that I thought she did, too. She offered only token resistance, sliding a mere inch or two away. We both were enjoying the contact.

Finally, however, she had all she could cope with and yelled at me in her deep, rejecting voice one of her usual scolding words: "Put–a–*what*! Put–a–*what*!" I had been reading how Bettelheim frequently asks his children the meaning of words and actions unfamiliar to him, so I said, "What does that mean, Karen?" She immediately stopped shouting, turned to me with a sweet expression, and said in a normal voice, "Put away!"

To end our session today, I carried Karen around and around the room, her head on my shoulder. I repeatedly told her what a good and pretty baby she was, and asked her if she were a good baby, answering for her. She thoroughly enjoyed my chatter, and chattered herself, not in words I could understand, but she did speak in a normal speech pattern and intonation. Just as we were about to leave for the lunchroom, I asked her once more if she were a good baby. "Karen!" she replied.

I had never heard her say her own name before.

February 11

After each session I leave a note for Tonia, telling her what Karen and I have done. Last week the note disappeared before Tonia returned from lunch, so today she told me to put it in her desk drawer.

In the drawer I found some instructions about the children. Karen, these notes instructed, is one of those in the class who cannot go to the bathroom by herself. Also, when she grimaces or shouts when asking for something—to be swung, for example—she is to be ignored and the request granted only after a ten-second interval. I also saw a list of words that she had said for another psychology student last week. At the bottom of the list the student had written, "Karen responded 58 times today."

Well, Karen *can* go to the bathroom on her own;

in fact, when she is with me, it must be on her own. Today, one of the foster grandmothers who work in Tonia's class came into our room to remind me that it was time for Karen to be taken to the bathroom. She utterly refused, hanging with all her might to the door as I tried to carry her out of the room. About fifteen minutes later, she casually wandered out into the hall, and we went to the bathroom together, on her initiative. Afterward, she turned on the water to "wash" her hands, which consisted of extending her fingertips to pinch at the cold stream of water.

As for her grimaces and shouts, I don't ignore them at all. I participate in them as much as I can. Just as Karen repeats some of my words, I repeat some of hers. When she shouts "Yo! Yo!" I shout "Yo! Yo!" I simply cannot believe that I am merely reinforcing Karen's shouting. I hope to be building a reciprocal relationship with her. When I shout back at her, or ask her what "Put–a–*what*" means, she knows I am entering her world a little bit and trying to understand it, however dimly.

Actually, I don't remember Karen shouting at all today. We had a good, good session. For long periods of time she sustained eye contact with me, and we had lengthy back-and-forth communication. She jabbered; she hummed; she laughed; she said her name a few times; she threw the apple across the room and up toward the light, always running lightly on her tiptoes. Whenever she began to twiddle the apple stem, I interfered: I grabbed it out of her hand, I attacked it with the carrot, I crawled around her on all fours. I kissed her cheek and neck with abandon. And Karen really enjoyed it! We are starting to *play* together!

I did not count the number of times Karen responded today.

February 13

Karen was out sick today. She has had a cold for quite a while.

February 18

One word for today: anger! Who knows why—perhaps because she has been sick, or at home too long, away from school too long. Perhaps a reason altogether different. Anyway, her anger made me acutely aware of my relationship with Karen. I see her for only two to three hours a week; aside from the few things Tonia tells me, I have no idea how or what Karen is doing the rest of the time. I have no idea what influence or carry-over she gets from our time together, although Tonia keeps assuring me that she is progressing.

Karen *was* angry today. We brought a brand new alphabet book with us from her classroom. Within a few minutes, Karen was carefully tearing holes in several pages, saying to me all the while, "Don't tear the book! Don't tear the book!" She also repeatedly pointed to a picture of an apple and shouted, "Orange! Orange!" Finally she hurled the book across the room, slapped her face, and kept up a stream of shouts and grunts.

I did not interfere with any of this behavior, save to kiss her face after she slapped it, which she allowed. I confess to being upset when she tore the new book, years of conditioning coming to the fore, but she was apparently rebelling against all the instructions and commands she is constantly subjected to, and further, feeling free enough to display her anger in front of me without fear of repercussion. I didn't want to betray her trust.

February 20

Tonia was full of Karen's progress today. She said Karen is starting to use personal pronouns—"I went swimming," "I want gum"—after some encouragement from Tonia. She also knows at least some of the days of the week; before I came this morning, she said, "Today is Wednesday."

I am very encouraged by all of this, since one of my basic aims with Karen, especially after reading Bettelheim, is to help her develop an idea of her own separate identity. Also, I always sing to her which day of the week it happens to be when I see her, and tell her exactly when I will return. In this way, maybe I can help her to have a sense of time periods relative to her own life.

However, I did not get much sense at all of this verbal progress during our session today. Monday's anger was gone, or possibly submerged; in its place was silence. She responded little to the books or fruit.

Only when I carried her to the window at our hour's end did I sense some change in Karen. She stood on the large sill, half leaning back into my arms, and really looked out the window. I talked about the sunshine, the trees, the birds, the clouds, and all the rest of what we could see. Karen said nothing, but she genuinely *listened*, and there was a sense of calm about her I have not often observed, and never for so long a time. I swung her around, her head leaning back into a patch of sunshine in the room. She squinted into it and her expression was that of a happy and peaceful child.

When it was time for lunch, Karen intently watched me restring my shoelaces. Just as I was finishing, she took the shoe away from me. I assumed she was going to take the string out again, but instead she wanted to do the last two holes! She strung them incorrectly, but I told her how very pleased I was and tied them as they were.

In the lunchroom, she bent down and touched my shoe in a gesture of farewell, as she sometimes does to say hello. It was the closest she has come to acknowledging my leaving; usually she ignores the whole issue and never looks at me once we have entered the lunchroom.

February 25

School was cancelled today because of a snowstorm.

February 27

When I arrived, Karen was sitting with the rest of the children listening to a record. She wanted to stay with them, it was clear, so I sat and watched. She turned around frequently to check on my presence.

Karen participated in the class's sing-along, not very loudly, it is true, but louder than several of the other children. At one point, the song called for them to get up and circle around a chair. Karen jumped up to participate, but by the time she had reached the designated chair, the song said to circle in the opposite direction and Karen was moving cross-current to the rest of the children. A foster grandmother grabbed her and forced her the other way. Karen resisted and began her grunting; the grandmother unloosed her with a momentarily hostile look.

As for progress, Tonia said Karen had thrown a rubber duck into the swimming pool this morning and then had laughed. Tonia had never heard her laugh before. And such a deep throaty laugh it is!

Before we began our time together in our room, Karen darted into the trampoline room and jumped vigorously for a few minutes. It was as if she were working off her frustration; she had sought to be physically active in the classroom, but had been thwarted because she went clockwise instead of counterclockwise.

As I reflected on our session today, I was amazed at how far Karen has come in our month together. Today not only were there no grunts, grimaces, "yo's," or "put–a–what's," but also the time spent in perseveration was practically nil and easily interrupted.

Most of the time Karen sat half in my arms, half on the window sill, and we jabbered at each other. She continues to repeat some of the words that I say, but now more and more she initiates words and letters that she likes, and then it is my turn to repeat them. For example, we shouted the letter *a* and the phrase "in here" back and forth innumerable times. She was very relaxed and playful, and as I was carrying her out the door at lunchtime, she suddenly touched a few strands of my hair and moved them off my forehead.

I am torn between initiating more structured activities and continuing this kind of friendly session, since just our jabbering and touching is obviously very beneficial to her.

March 4

Last night I dreamed I ran into Karen's family—Karen, her father and brother, both of whom I have seen at the school where the father works, although they have no idea who I am. In the dream, we are standing at a sidewalk intersection; the sunshine is very bright and crystalline. Karen darts out from behind her father, her face full of joy. We are ecstatic at seeing each other.

Today we had a restless session together. Forced to vacate the room we usually use because of workmen making repairs, we wandered around the building and finally ended up in the small-fry classroom. Karen would have nothing to do with any attempts to work on the alphabet. She played with two musical toys the entire time, her back toward me. I contented myself with caressing her back and keeping up a stream of chatter, which she probably tuned right out.

I noticed that Karen refused to use the toilet twice today, both times evidently because the deposits of the prior user were still visible. Maybe this is connected with her habit of running from one toilet to another, flushing each one. I had assumed she enjoyed this activity, even though she does run from the noise of the flush, which is considerable. Perhaps she does it more to get rid of all the dirt.

March 5

I found out some interesting things about Karen's older brother Tommy today. I have seen him at all hours of the day with his father and wondered about his schooling. It seems that Tommy is six years old and presently doing high school level work in arithmetic; he does long-division problems in his head, etc.

March 6

The words for today's session were "anger" and "sadness." It all started when I carried Karen to the window so we could once again look out at the clouds and sky. She banged her palm tentatively on the glass pane, first gently, then harder and harder, and then finally she took the small wooden music box she had brought with her from the classroom and smacked it against the glass with all her might. She was perfectly capable of breaking the window and I could not let that happen, so I carried her protesting body away.

Again and again she wound up her toy to make music, only to start whining after a few minutes. At first she was content to throw the music box across the floor to show her anger; then she began to slap herself and then to hit herself on the head with the wooden toy.

All this time I was verbalizing for her that she

felt both angry and sad, and that she really felt like breaking something. I also shielded her head as best I could from her blows, since she could have done herself serious damage. I told her, "Don't hurt yourself," and she repeated this admonition to herself in a distressed and tearful voice.

Suddenly her anger dissipated into sadness, and I could sense a feeling of fantastic frustration inside her, something trying desperately to become unloosed. She rolled on the floor, kicking and crying. It took a while for the tears to make their way past her grunts and moans, but come they finally did.

We lay together on the floor and she sought the comfort of my body, holding on to me with arms and legs. During a few moments of acute crying, she reached down into her pants and touched her vagina for a little self-comfort. She looked up at me through her tears for my reaction. I smiled and told her I understood how good that must feel.

We missed lunchtime, but a friendly aide brought her lunch bag upstairs to us. Eating calmed her. Head propped on my knees, she munched bread and cookies. She even spelled out her name, which was printed on her lunch bag.

I did not want to be the one to end this session, but after a long morning I had to go to the bathroom, even if Karen didn't. From the toilet, I heard her making sad noises, and then I heard her run back down the hall into her classroom. When I peeked in a few minutes later, she was dancing on tiptoe to music from the record player, her face calm. I called a good-bye to her and quietly left.

March 11 and 13

These two sessions have run together in my mind, because we spent them both in the trampoline room, jumping on the giant air mattress as well as the trampoline. The room was so noisy with the other children using it that we couldn't exchange too much verbal communication, but she was quite physical with me and initiated lots of touching. For the first time, I tickled her belly full force while we were on the air mattress, and she laughed and laughed!

The adults who surround her in her school environment continue to surprise and upset me. A teacher I had met briefly a few days ago today said to me, right within earshot of Karen, "Do you know what I'd do if this kid were in my class? I'd spank her bottom everyday!"

Also today, while waiting for Karen to finish her milk-and-cookie snack, I saw how, as soon as Tonia leaves the room for her own break, the foster grandmothers' will-to-power springs into action. "All right now, let's learn some table manners! One hand on the lap while eating!" The paper cups are flimsy and heavy with milk; spills are inevitable. "Mikie, why do you always spill what you eat! What a mess!" And so it goes.

From Tonia I learned that Karen's mother is noticing her progress. It seems Karen is responding to her physically a little and they are working on numbers together.

Besides Tommy, there is also a nine-month-old baby in the family. The mother hopes "*this* child will be normal."

Tonia also told me that Karen has had a succession of baby-sitters since the mother works full time. One was a homesick Korean girl who wrote letters constantly and left Karen to her own devices, even allowing her outdoors unwatched as a toddler. The present sitter is an old woman who has to be roused from sleep to claim Karen off the school bus.

Week of March 18

Spring Vacation. I spent it at my parents' house and was with my niece for most of each day. At three and one-half, Jessica does easily so many things which Karen is struggling toward! I find I have so much more freedom of action with Jessica, too; I do not have to be so hesitant or restrained. This interlude with a normally functioning child invigorated me for working with Karen, although the inevitable comparisons made me realize how far Karen has to come.

March 25

Karen and I were so happy to see each other again! She pulled me down the hall to our room so fast that I didn't have time to get any toys and had to return for them. Actually, we now are using props less and less and attend more and more to each other.

I chased her all over the room, grabbed her, tickled her. She laughed and laughed, her deep laugh sometimes so breathless that I had to keep watch to reassure myself she was laughing and not crying.

Today a new game developed with my shoelaces and some of the fruit toys. Karen took them one by one into the hall and dropped them down the stairwell. I wanted to stop her, because I knew the teachers down below would not approve, but her delight was so great I didn't have the heart. How good it is to watch her play!

After a few minutes of hurtling carrots and potatoes, we went downstairs, Karen still chortling, to retrieve everything. Karen ran into the little children's classroom, where we had spent some time another day. She read the letters off some alphabet blocks and then settled down to play with a jack-in-the-box. After a bit, she began whining and grimacing, and then sobbing.

At this point Mrs. B. (the teacher who would spank Karen's bottom every day) told Karen to be quiet, so-and-so was taking a nap. She was rather nasty about it, too. I carried the protesting Karen out, without a word to Mrs. B.

March 27

I was informed first thing today that Mrs. B. wants neither me nor Karen in her classroom anymore. Such hostility Karen is capable of inspiring!

Tonia also told me some stories about this school's teachers and administrators punishing unruly children with a yardstick, whether their unruliness is connected with their emotional disturbance, cerebral palsy, or mental retardation.

Today was such a beautiful warm spring day that I couldn't abide spending it in the stuffy school building, so Karen and I went for a walk. We walked around the block several times, Karen sometimes in my arms, sometimes walking beside me holding my hand. She seemed fearful at first, recoiling from the leaves and flowers I showed her, but gradually she loosened up. At one point she even dared stomp in a mud puddle and pull out clumps of grass with both hands. As we walked we sang "This Old Man"; she knows quite a few of the words.

We also spent some time in the playground on a jungle gym. Here, too, Karen was tentative at first, but she soon became bolder in her movements, and even said "Superman!" It is good for her to climb and sit on the bars; she can gain some facility with her body, which is clumsy from disuse. Also, she needs to use both hands to hold on to the equipment, which keeps finger twiddling to a minimum. All in all, it was a peaceful and invigorating session out in the sunshine.

While sitting on the toilet before lunch, Karen spread her legs for me to view her genitals and began playing with herself. If a foster grandmother had walked past us then, we really would have been in trouble!

April 1

Today we spent the whole hour outside on the playground. Other children were using the equipment, too, and Karen had a hard time sharing, especially the swings. She smacked whoever might be on "her" swing, even if there were other swings available for her to use.

I am sure Karen has gained a little weight in the past few months; her face is fuller and she seems taller, too. She is entering a new phase, I think—a vocal, playful one. She laughs quite often now, especially at the words "washing machine, machine, machine" which we say together, and then I follow up by tickling her.

In fact, all I had to do today to stop her finger twiddling was to initiate this play and she would immediately laugh and become active again. She also has started yowling very loudly, but it changes so easily and quickly into just as loud laughter, that I take it to be a good sign of healthy expression.

Today more than ever before Karen really grabbed me and hugged me around the neck. She closed her eyes as I peppered her face with kisses and held my hands around her waist. It is good for us to be outside; the sky is so much more friendly than the school ceilings.

On the way into lunch Karen triumphantly pounded through a mud puddle.

April 2

I was pedaling my bicycle to school early this morning when I spied a small blue school bus about a block away, two passengers in it. Even at that distance I had no trouble recognizing Karen. She sat so small and straight—staring, self-insulated, and alone. I waved as the bus passed me, but she did not see.

April 3

Karen continues to delight in throwing things. Lately, according to Tonia, she has begun throwing toys out the second-floor window, laughing heartily all the while. The women on the first floor complain, naturally. Today Karen was again throwing all the fruits down the stairwell until we heard a sharp voice, "Who *is* that throwing things?"

We had to stay inside today since it was a rainy morning. Karen was a marvel of good, responsive humor. She understands chasing games now and runs from me, several times even hiding as I stalked her.

When I think of those beginning days when we sat on the floor the whole time! Now I am exhausted by lunchtime. I am happy to see her so active and vigorous.

April 8

Today was snowy and cold and we again had to stay inside. It becomes more and more difficult to deal with Karen indoors because of her ever increasing energy. She does not want to look at books—in fact, in the classroom she rips them up if left unattended—nor even concentrate on a toy. She wants to spring forth all her vigor at once. I must chase her, tickle her, repeat "washing machine, machine, machine" ad infinitum while she emits a variety of chuckles and chortles.

I can no longer even bring our bag of fruits and vegetables with us, since I know they will be thrown enthusiastically down the stairs and we will be chastised. She is forced, therefore, to limit her throwing game to my shoelaces, the loss of which I steel myself to every session; miraculously I have thus far always been able to find them.

April 10

Still too cold to go outdoors and I anticipated mayhem, but Karen was in a fairly quiet mood. We sang quite a bit. Our theme song has switched from Mulberry Bush to This Old Man. I leave out the key words for Karen to insert:

"This old man, he played . . ."

"One!"

"He played knick-knack on my . . ."

"Thumb!"

As when she obstinately calls an orange an apple, she sometimes teases me with the numbers of this song. I carefully hold up three fingers at the appropriate stanza, and she, just as carefully and with due thought, shouts out, "Five!" I must then respond with a "washing machine, machine, machine" tickle. Perhaps the fact that Karen's mother is working with her on numbers is irrelevant here, but I also noticed that a favorite book of hers had the part of a page which contained a cluster of numbers carefully torn and neatly folded back in Karen's trademark tearing style. The rest of the page was left untouched.

She reaches out for my arms to be hugged or carried or swung so often now I *almost* take it for granted, just as she now seems to accept my kisses and caresses *almost* with nonchalance.

April 15 and 17

Although the weather has been warm this week, we stayed inside at Karen's insistence. She seemingly likes our customary, inside playing patterns;

outside, too, there are so many distractions, while inside we usually have each other's full attention.

Karen continues to progress. Her body becomes increasingly more at her command; I am surprised to remember her awkward, pained posturing of two months ago. She now jumps on the trampoline with great confidence, even by herself, bouncing on her knees and bottom. She even turns a few hesitant somersaults. Moreover, we have been going up and down the stairs so often to retrieve my shoelaces that she can negotiate them without holding my hand, something she could not do even a few weeks ago. In fact, she now attempts two stairs at a time!

But the biggest achievement of all this week turned out to be something quite tangible: Karen's first painting—energetic swirls of red and blue, with some drips of green. As Tonia was showing it to me, a foster grandmother interrupted to say, no, her *first* painting was in the back room. We followed her there, and saw circles of blue and red painted directly on an easel. The grandmother said Karen had put on and buttoned the painting smock all by herself (another first), before executing this, her first art work.

I assumed the paper painting would be given to Karen's mother, but Tonia said I should have it. Selfishly, I did not refuse. It is already framed, and hanging on my apartment wall.

April 22

Some more "firsts" today. Tonia said Karen had been saying my name all morning after being told that I was coming to see her. I hoped she would say it again, but of course when asked, silence was the response. Karen rarely calls me anything to my face, but when she does it is "teacher," which she also calls Tonia.

Also, when I said it was lunchtime, Karen shouted out "Bye-bye!" I have always hated our partings in the lunchroom, but today she kept eye contact with me as I left and repeated "bye-bye" several times.

Karen's aggression, of which I have been aware almost from the beginning, is manifesting itself more and more in the classroom, and in an ambiguous manner. Tonia says she hits the children quite frequently now, saying all the while, "Don't hit! Don't hit!" and then presents her own hand to Tonia to be hit back in punishment. Needless to say, Tonia does not comply.

April 24

Today both Karen and I were very relaxed and playful. For the last few sessions we have had the trampoline room all to ourselves, which allows us to make all the noise we want without feeling guilty about it. We jump together for long stretches, shouting "this old man" and "washing machine" at the top of our lungs.

Karen's intermittent whining of a few weeks ago has completely stopped; in its place is unadulterated, joyous laughter. Since she likes me to carry her in my arms as we jump, I get tired and frequently lie down on the trampoline to rest. At these times I tickle Karen and we wrestle a bit.

Today as she was lying, laughing, in my arms, she looked up and said, "Love you." Actually, it came out more like a "lub you," but the thought was clearly there.

On the way down to the lunchroom, we stopped on the stairs while I put Karen's socks on for her. When I was done, she said "Thank you!" ("Thang you.") It is always such a surprise when she speaks so appropriately.

We were late for lunch because Karen took a fifteen-minute bowel movement, one small piece deposited in each of several toilets.

When we did get to the lunchroom, I noticed that the foster grandmother who now feeds Karen had cut her sandwich into bite-sized pieces, meat included. Perhaps Karen is eating her whole lunch these days; certainly she is eating more somewhere, because she has gained weight. Once again, we exchanged bye-byes as I left.

April 29–May 1–May 3

I went to see Karen three mornings this week. Each day some time was spent on the trampoline and some time in the bathroom, putting seats up, putting them down, flushing, depositing her bowel movement in several favorite bowls, and finally admiring her little bottom and rectum in the full-length mirror.

I tried at each session this week to give Karen a picture vocabulary test which yields an IQ score. For one of my courses I have to test a child at the Center, and I decided to see what I could get on Karen. On the first attempt, she correctly pointed to a cow and a bus when I asked her to identify them, but the next word was "baby," and she completely blocked and refused to have anything more to do with the picture book. Subsequent attempts were also complete failures and sent Karen into finger twiddling and postures of rejection.

Tonia had filled out a behavior-rating scale on Karen for me, and as we went over it together, I realized my view of her progress is certainly one-sided. What we have achieved in our relationship has carried over to her other activities, but only to a limited extent, and then only with those people she likes, that is, those who provide her with affection and stimulation and not always with commands and instructions. For all the other people in her world, she remains in isolation. For example, when Tonia was absent from the classroom for an afternoon, Karen kept picking one place on her arm until it bled.

Karen's mother told Tonia recently that Karen had always gone into her room to play by herself, and so she had assumed that Karen preferred to be alone and made no attempt to follow her. Apparently, the mother felt rejected and so herself withdrew.

To return to this week's sessions, I feel that Karen is entering a stage of testing the limits with me. Never have I felt so at odds with myself over what I should do with Karen, especially as I watch her flushing toilets systematically for ten minutes straight, or running back and forth, back and forth, through ankle-deep mud puddles when we venture outside. She wears such a look of blind insistence at these times that, short of carrying her away, I am unable to interrupt.

I am less inclined to interrupt her toilet activities, as they have recently been culminating in bowel movements, and who can know what demons she must exorcise before she feels comfortable around toilets, but I do stop her water play after letting her indulge for a few muddy moments.

If her total atmosphere were permissive, it would be different, but mostly her environment is so much the opposite—and Karen must function in it after I leave. As it is, we are continually getting into trouble with the grandmothers when I bring her into lunch late, muddy, barefoot, and with pants all twisted around from being rolled up and down so many times.

Today I found out that Karen's birthday was just a few weeks ago. She is now five years old.

May 6

After last week's frustrations, I rather hesitantly went to visit Karen today. And what a glorious session it turned out to be! When I first entered her classroom, I noticed that two more of her paintings were taped up—one labeled "Karen's first watercolor" and the other "Karen's third painting."

Also, Tonia was happy to report that Karen's hitting has almost disappeared and that she now jumps off the slide in the gym room as a trick to show the other children, with whom she can now take turns on the equipment.

Karen was very verbal with me today, and I felt that our whole time together was productive. She immediately led me into the trampoline room, said "Take off your shoes" as always, and then when she noticed me struggling to remove my sweatshirt, added "Take off your shirt!" We sang and jumped and tickled and hugged. Then she said, "Get down?" So we did.

On our way out, she put on her shoes and got a gleam in her eyes as she spied my shiny white shoe-laces. (Last week she finally managed to lose my old brown ones.) As she started to pull them out of my shoes with twiddling fingers, I stopped her, saying we weren't going to do that today. To my surprise she stopped, and then waited for me to put on and tie my sneakers before she ran off down the hall.

In the gym room she wanted to "climb the ladder." I held her while she groped for the overhead horizontal bars. Soon I started releasing her for a few seconds and she was able to support her own weight. After a few minutes, she hung on to me and the bar at the same time and then said, "Let go of me!" Proper pronoun usage and non-echolalic as well!

We didn't even have a fuss at lunchtime. When I told her it was time, she ran right to her socks and shoes, said "Put your socks on," and put them on without any help. Since she had gone to the bathroom soon after I came, we even made it through the row of toilets in the basement with only a few token flushes.

I now wait in the lunchroom until she says bye-bye and sustains eye contact while she says it; today I got a prompt bye-bye and a big smile besides.

May 8

I was really looking forward to this session, but I found Karen's classroom empty. A grandmother said all the children were using the university's gymnasium facilities.

May 13

At last! Karen's language usage has improved noticeably even from last week. I have taught her to say "Carry me" when she wants to be lifted, and she generally says what it is that she wants to do, if only in two or three word phrases—"jump," "drink of water," "get down."

Today she initiated quite a little discussion revolving around "Do you want to sit down?" I could not tell whether she was using the pronoun correctly or not, whether she was making a genuine inquiry or merely repeating the sentence as it had been addressed to her, but we exchanged it (a long one, for her) back and forth many times.

During a toilet flushing binge, a very old foster grandmother, a nun actually, came into the bathroom. She always mispronounces Karen's name and once told us to leave the room where we were playing, grabbing a toy out of Karen's hands. Today I looked at this woman and then at Karen, and damned if Karen wasn't mugging a face to look like a perfect caricature of this wrinkled old woman! She only held it for a moment or two, and then said "glasses."

"Yes, Karen, she's wearing glasses."

"Wearing glasses."

I always try to incorporate Karen's words and phrases into complete sentences, but it is easy to forget this procedure and only repeat the words you are sure she can understand and will repeat. This verbal laziness happens, too, when a mother understands so well what her child means that she allows him or her to communicate without expressing whole thoughts. Karen's language development is, I would think, on the level of a two or three year old. Sometimes it truly frightens me to realize she is five.

The classroom was empty for a few minutes before lunch, and I grabbed paper and crayon to retrieve Karen's wandering attention. She put my hand to the paper and spelled her name out for me to write. (Tonia later told me Karen has learned to gain her mother's attention by spelling her name and other words to her. The mother said she can help Karen academically, but that she is no good at playing.)

Then Karen said "Draw a car" and "Draw a house," and identified the door and windows for me. Unfortunately, we were interrupted by the other children at this point and had to stop.

The foster grandmothers now make no effort to disguise their distaste for me. They constantly give me commands about Karen's shoes and socks, her state of cleanliness, and on and on, which I do my best to ignore. Today they swiped the crayon box out from under my nose and had it locked up in the supply cabinet before I even realized it; the drawing paper was in the wastebasket two minutes after I had drawn on it. Such an insane insistence on tidiness!

May 15 and 17

Tonia is now convinced that Karen is a genius! She can spell and recognize more words than any other child in the class. I am glad Karen's intelligence is beginning to show and be appreciated.

Karen and I did some more drawing during our first session this week; or rather, I drew as she directed me—apples, cars, houses, and lips. Tonia has started drawing for her, too.

Friday turned out to be such a hot, humid day that we didn't last very long on the trampoline. Karen spent a good bit of our hour playing with the water in the bathroom sink. It seemed almost a regressive day; perhaps because of the heat, or the cough she has developed, whatever, Karen did a lot of finger twiddling, and her laughter often turned into whining or grimaces.

This week I have noticed that Karen has begun to form a friendship with a brain-damaged boy whose name is Stevie. Twice this week, once in the hall and once in the lunchroom, I heard them exchange the communication "Aw-tee," which seemed mutually understandable and satisfying to them. Tonia also mentioned to me that when Stevie recently fell and hurt himself, Karen was solicitous and surprisingly tender toward him.

May 20 and 22

This was an important week for Karen. Monday she gave me a tentative shove, and I immediately encouraged her, saying "Hit me. It's all right. Hit me as hard as you want." So she did, pushing me into the wall both from in front and behind for several minutes.

Later, as I carried her down to lunch, I said to her, "Give me a kiss, Karen?" and she responded with a pucker right on my lips! I was surprised, to say the least. Today she both hit and kissed me for the first time!

On Wednesday, Tonia told me Karen has completely stopped hitting the other children, to the relief and delight of everyone. Tonia has also started encouraging Karen to hit her, instead of anyone else.

Again on Wednesday Karen pushed me around, saying as she did so, "Don't hit! Don't hit!" I assured her it was all right to hit me. A few minutes later, while sitting in my arms, she suddenly beat fiercely on my chest and even put her hands around my throat. It took me a while to be genuinely pleased at this emotional expression!

May 29

Last night I dreamed I was walking around the Center, Karen in my arms, and we were talking to each other in complete and intelligible sentences. I thought how wonderful it was that we could finally communicate with each other so fully.

June 5

Karen's school semester is over, so I have had to decide what I want to do over the summer. Since I do not want to miss three months of working with Karen, I decided to contact her family and try and see her at home.

After talking with Mrs. Ling twice on the phone during the week, I went to visit Karen at her home this morning. Mrs. Ling was at work, but Mr. Ling was home, along with brother Tommy and the baby Theodore, aged fourteen months. He watched for a few minutes as Karen and I ran around the backyard. She was somewhat astounded to see me and shouted loudly, to the embarrassment of Mr. Ling, who tried to control her and succeeded only in precipitating finger twiddling.

Tommy followed us around after we went into the house, handing me lists of words Karen can spell, which Mrs. Ling had prepared for me, and telling me how he works with high-degree mathematical equations. He also asked me to write down any suggestions I might have about Karen. Karen continually smacked him on the back. He has been instructed by his mother to ignore these attacks, and he did, but several times he told me he couldn't take much more.

Karen jumped up and down on her mother's bed, and we wrestled a bit on this home version of a trampoline. We also ate a snack, with Karen sitting in my lap; then we wrote some words and drew some pictures together. Karen held on to my hand as I drew and sometimes scribbled by herself. The next step will surely be for her to tackle letters completely on her own. She seems to enjoy this activity very much and does it with her mother also.

As I left, Karen cried and came to hug me goodbye, saying my name through her tears. I was touched to hear her say my name at last.

June 19

Tonight I rode my bicycle over to the Ling house and met Mrs. Ling for the first time. She drove Karen and me to a nearby park, and while Karen played on the swings and slides, she and I had time to talk and compare notes on her daughter. My optimism was heartening to her, since most of the people she has talked with (except for Tonia) consider Karen hopeless.

From the many things we discussed, what struck me most was that she said she wanted to watch me "for techniques to use with Karen" and that she remarked, "Karen gets more love from you than she does from me."

Karen herself was a joy, plainly happy to be in the company of both her mother and her friend. She laughed, hopped, and even sang all by herself in a beautiful little soprano voice. She behaved differently, more openly, than I have been accustomed to seeing; whether this difference is due to progress or simply to being at home as opposed to the Center, I do not know.

She was very responsive and obedient to her mother; she spelled every damn word she was asked. Mrs. Ling joked that Karen could win a spelling bee even if she couldn't talk. Karen was very affectionate with me physically. I can only hope Mrs. Ling picks up on this "technique"; not once during my two-hour visit did they touch each other.

My husband stopped by the Ling house to ride home with me; I was happy that he and Karen finally met. Mr. Ling told him he was afraid Karen might be brain-damaged.

The whole family escorted us to our bicycles when we were ready to leave, Mr. and Mrs. Ling entreating Karen to wave good-bye to us. Finally, she came to stand by my side and waved at her parents!

June 26

This visit, my third to Karen's house, was spent entirely in the backyard. Karen was quite affectionate, touching the buttons ("buttons?") on my blouse and lifting up my hair to examine it intently. After touching my long hair, she put her hand up to her own short-cropped hair style, and seemed puzzled.

John came again to meet me and seated himself close to the swing set where Karen and I were swinging together. She immediately hid coyly behind my back, peeking her eyes around me to look at him. I could tell she wanted and enjoyed his attention; at the same time, his close presence made her nervous, and she frequently bent over to twiddle her shoe buckle, something she had not done before during this visit.

She has learned how to force herself to cough. When I first arrived tonight, she did it frequently. Later, she continued coughing to attract John's attention as I was carrying her around the yard and he was talking to Mrs. Ling at some distance from us.

Karen is attending a camp during the mornings this summer. She also sees a speech therapist for daily twenty-minute periods. The therapist is working on incorporating Karen's growing vocabulary into sentence patterns and is involving both Karen and her mother in word and number games to be played on Karen's fingers.

July 3

When I first met Karen six months ago, I could never have dreamed that tonight would have been possible. Back then I felt successful when I could hold her attention for more than a few consecutive minutes or caress her cheek without her turning away with grunts and yowls. Tonight Karen and her mother came to visit me in my apartment, and "shy" would be the most apt description of her behavior, not "disturbed" or "bizarre."

I had never before observed Karen in surroundings completely new and strange to her, so I did not know what to expect when I went outside to greet them. Confidently Karen held my hand and clomped up the stairs to my apartment.

Before I opened the door, I told her we had a kitty cat. "Kitty cat?" When we got inside and Karen saw the cat, she was afraid and pulled the ends of her mouth as far as she could, but I could see her fear was mixed with curiosity. I locked the cat in the bedroom until she felt more relaxed. Later on, she went into the bedroom and pointed at him, pushing me toward him so I would pet him. But even with coaxing she refused to touch him herself. They circled each other warily all evening. They are much alike, these two!

While John and Mrs. Ling talked, Karen and I played on the living room floor. I drew pictures on her command and even got her to direct the pen in circles by herself. She kept part of her body always in touch with mine, constantly changing position to be sitting on my legs or across my back. Often she did it offhandedly, backing into me as if by accident. At least she has lost her old fears of physical contact. I am still surprised and moved by it.

I also showed Karen her painting, framed and hanging on the wall. Her face immediately shone as she shouted, "Blue! Green! Red!" I am sure she recognized it as her own.

Toward the end of the evening Karen went into the bedroom and stood looking at the bed. I encouraged her to get on it, so she said, "Take off your shoes," took off hers, and lay down with her small dark face on my pillow. I lay down next to her and we hugged and tickled.

July 10

Mrs. Ling again brought Karen to my apartment to visit. Karen was nervous and upset at the beginning, perhaps because they had visited another friend before coming. It took me at least half an hour to calm her down so that she would sit in my arms and respond at all.

The kitty cat again fascinated her, and after much maneuvering and many grunts and groans, she managed to pet him—not once, but twice! This victory brought applause from the rest of us.

Karen discovered our bathroom for the first time and while jumping up and down on the scales, guided my hand to flush the toilet two or three times. Her mother called from the other room for her to stop, and Karen obediently went back into the bedroom, but for the next ten minutes said repeatedly, "Don't play with that!"

July 18

Tonight it was our turn to visit the Lings. Before Karen and I went outside to play on the swing set and tricycle, we sat at the table with paper and pen. It turned out to be a day of breakthrough! She pushed my hand away from the pen and drew all by herself, not only wild scribbles which at times ripped through the paper but also letters (to spell "house") and a few numbers and a hand wearing a wristwatch!

In response to her father's persistent questioning, Karen says "My name is Karen" and "I am five years old." This is heartening to him, because it shows she is capable of understanding, but to me she sounds so soulless and robotlike when forced to talk.

July 20

The Lings invited us on a picnic today; we went to a park some miles out of town. It gave me a chance to observe Karen in new surroundings with her entire family and also amidst other, normal children.

On the ride out to the park, Karen sat beside her mother in the back seat and I turned around from the front seat often enough to notice Mrs. Ling touching Karen's face and teasing her in a gentle voice. Karen was altogether silent and I saw her push her mother's hand away once, but she remained sitting glued to her side.

Once at the park, the first activity was swimming

in a small lake. I took Karen in the water, while John observed from the beach how all the mothers were staring at us, no doubt wondering if Karen were my adopted and/or retarded child.

Karen dogpaddled on her own for a few seconds and floated while lying across my back. For the rest of the hour or so we spent in the water, she jumped off a cement block (used to secure a large slide), clambered back on with my help and jumped off, again and again and again. Other children would sometimes want to play the same game, and at first Karen would hit them. I had to restrain her in the water to make her take proper turns. After a while she got the hang of sharing a little better. She would give the child jumping ahead of her only a gentle shove of assistance.

The other children playing all around us in the water were Karen's age or a year or two older; a few were curious about her.

"Is it a boy or a girl?"

"Is she your kid?"

Again it came as a shock to me how verbal children of that age are, as compared with Karen. She only said "water" and "jump" and "eleven," which number for some reason she shouted gleefully as she hit the water each time. Occasionally she said, "What's the matter?" when a child spoke directly to her.

Getting her out of the water precipitated a full-blown tantrum. Karen screamed and cried harder than I have ever heard her. I had to carry her out of the water and across the beach of staring people.

When we all sat down to eat at a picnic table,

Karen was more subdued but still upset. When her mother tried to get her to eat a hot dog, Karen again erupted into cries and screams. Mrs. Ling spoke *very* sharply to her, and Mr. Ling gave her a poke in the back as he passed by.

Sitting across the table from them, I was able to see everyone's expression. Karen's gave me a quick stab of pain. The word "sadness" does not even begin to express what I saw in her face. Mrs. Ling then told me that Karen sometimes works herself up into such a fury that she vomits, but that if she is told to stop sternly enough, she stops and stops fast.

During the rest of the afternoon Karen played on the merry-go-round, the small pushable kind, which either I or John or Mrs. Ling or even chubby, unathletic Tommy pushed. Sometimes there was a mob of other children hanging on for "free" rides, sometimes only one or two, but always there was Karen, sitting silently in the middle.

Several times while I was sitting, resting, at the picnic table I noticed she was all alone and went to give her a push and talk to her. Once, to excuse myself from the group of grown-ups, I mentioned that Karen was by herself. Mr. Ling said, "Oh, just forget her. Forget her." I know he meant for me to relax and not worry, but I was sorry anyway that he had said it.

Again, the other children playing around us talked to Karen. Although she did not respond to them, I wondered if being around normal gabby children more might not be a good inducement for her to increase her speech. The children at the Center have learned to ignore her for the most part.

On the way home, Mrs. Ling worked on getting Karen to stop twiddling her fingers and to stop saying "apples." "If you don't *see* any apples, then don't *say* apples." Her premise seems to be that if she can stop Karen's "bizarre manifestations," then everything will be all right. Perhaps.

When we arrived at our apartment, Karen leaned forward from the back seat. I asked her for a kiss and she surprised me with one on the lips. I wonder if her parents were surprised as well.

August 8

I had to wait two weeks before visiting Karen again at her home. I was ill one week, the Ling children the next. By the end of the second week, I was dreaming about Karen almost every night. In most of these dreams, Karen was learning to speak in sentences and I was delighted at how much better we were able to communicate with each other. The last dream I had about her before seeing her again had Karen crouching in a corner, surprising me by her smallness. Her body was stiff, as if made of cardboard. When I called her to me and put my arms around her, she relaxed completely.

My dreams were optimistic, my conscious thoughts not so. Coincidentally, Mrs. Ling echoed them tonight: "Sometimes I get so frightened she will always be like this." I could only tell her what I tell myself for reassurance: that such fears are tenable only if Karen stops growing, but in fact she continues to grow.

"But if only she would learn faster. She is so far behind."

I guess we have to learn to forget external time. Karen is growing to her own, internal time rhythms.

Our time tonight was considerably shortened by a television special which everyone wanted to watch. Karen bounced on and off my knee as we sat on the floor together. She kept repeating her favorite word of the day, "morning."

Before the program, however, Mrs. Ling showed me what she has been teaching Karen. For one thing, she has taught her to use a pair of children's scissors and to cut paper with them. She also draws pictures of large bananas and apples and has Karen color them, preferably with the appropriate crayon and within the lines. Some drawings Mrs. Ling leaves unfinished and has Karen draw the closure lines. Karen performs all these tasks well, with a little prodding, and also prints the numbers from one to five.

I think Mrs. Ling did indeed take note of Karen's kissing me at the end of our picnic trip. Tonight Mrs. Ling and I were standing side by side and Karen came up to me and said, "Kiss Mommy." By the time I got her steered over to Mommy, she was saying "Kiss teacher," per Mrs. Ling's instructions! In the confusion, I don't remember who actually received the kiss.

August 15 and 19

I was able to visit with Karen twice in five days, so the visits have run together in my mind. Both times were spent at her house, mostly outside on the swing set and tricycle.

During the few minutes we did spend with paper and pencil, I was impressed by her complete sentences: "Let's draw a rabbit." "This is a take-a-bath." A take-a-bath, naturally, is a bathtub. A turn-the-water-on is a faucet.

Karen's mood seems happy lately, but I never know how she is when I am not with her, and sometimes her good humor seems contrived or forced. Several times this week I have tickled her until she was laughing really hard, and then have had to leave her alone for a few minutes. Upon my return, she would still be lying on her stomach, still laughing, but it was empty laughter—all noise and no soul. I pulled her up to look in her face; it was absolutely expressionless.

The state of our leavetakings has regressed to the point where Karen simply runs away when I tell her good-bye. When pressed by her parents, she says, "Say bye-bye." This response frustrates them no end. "Don't say 'say bye-bye,' Karen, say 'bye-bye!'" I know very well Karen *can* say good-bye and know what she is saying; we were doing very well at the Center with the same problem.

A concept of Bettelheim's strikes me anew: a child with an impoverished view of his or her own self cannot help but be retarded in social development. One possible explanation for Karen's speech, consisting as it does mostly of repetitions of commands directed at her all day, is that she will not let herself be aware of what *she* wants, only what others demand of her.

September 6

Events again conspired against us, so that another two weeks had to pass before I next saw

Karen. Tonight she and her mother spent an hour or so at my apartment. Since Mrs. Ling and I are becoming better acquainted, we have more and more things to discuss and I become hopelessly divided when the three of us are alone together. (John now works evenings.) I cannot help but feel I am being rude when I am paying attention to one at the exclusion of the other. Karen, of course, suffers most from this situation, as she immediately wanders off to twiddle her fingers when I talk to her mother.

Another problem is that Mrs. Ling, being ridiculously protective of my three-month-old pregnancy, does not allow Karen to crawl over my body, as she so delights in doing. As soon as she sits on my lap or wants to crawl on my back, Mrs. Ling tells her sharply, "Sha-lai! Sha-lai!" which means "get down!" in Chinese. Karen becomes upset and shouts "Sha-lai!" for the next ten minutes, along with "Don't play piggyback!"

Karen brought along one of her toy balls today and we spent some time playing catch. From a clumsy beginning at the start of the summer when we played in the backyard, Karen now catches the ball with only a few misses and understands the concept of throwing the ball to someone else in turn. She used to run off with the ball whenever it was tossed to her. Also, she says "catch the ball" and "throw the ball."

Karen has again started school at the Center. Unfortunately, Tonia has left the school and Karen has a new teacher, Mrs. Shott. When Mrs. Ling went to meet her, Mrs. Shott suggested that Karen go to the Mental Health Clinic for some psychiatric help. Mrs. Ling told me they probably will not go, since they tried it last year for a few expensive sessions. Apparently some family therapy was initiated, but Mrs. Ling felt it was of no use. She says she knows what is wrong with Karen—that as a child who came second into the family, she had been deprived of stimulation in infancy, when she most needed it. The task now, as Mrs. Ling sees it, is to make up for all the stimulation which was never given, most profitably in one-to-one relationships.

September 9

This morning I went to the Center with the intention of meeting the new teacher and setting up a time for seeing Karen. Since I need time alone with Karen, I felt that one morning a week at the school plus the time at home with her would give us more room in which to make some progress.

Mrs. Shott was giving the children some motor tests when I arrived. Karen recognized me and smiled, but knew better than to approach me right away, as the children were all lined up against the wall. Part of the test involved catching and throwing a ball, skills I knew very well Karen had, but I watched her resist to the utmost displaying them on the teacher's command.

Mrs. Shott is older than Tonia, perhaps in her late thirties, tall and heavy, with a determined, not too friendly, face. After a few minutes she came over to find out who I was. She told me Karen was doing very well in school and that her socialization had much improved since the addition of several more little girls to the class this year. She said all this is such a tone of personal achievement that I began to wonder if I would be able to work with her as easily as with the unassuming Tonia.

Mrs. Shott went on to say that I would need permission from the school's director before I could see Karen, the policy having been changed since last semester. A few minutes later she amended this to say she would talk it over with the director herself and give me their decision when I came in next week. Of course, I could only work with Karen if I would not be interfering with the class in any way, and I must coordinate my activities with hers. In fact, perhaps I should start by working with Karen on this very motor test.

For the moment, then, it was left at that. I was to return next week to hear their decision. Everyone else left the room, but Karen remained behind to be with me. I was so happy to have a few minutes alone with her before lunchtime that I disregarded caution, and let her climb on me for a piggyback ride.

We couldn't have been alone for more than thirty seconds when Mrs. Shott came back into the room and took Karen from my back, saying that while she had observed Karen during the summer, she had only been her teacher for a week and a half, and so must take her away from me so she wouldn't become upset. Karen was indeed upset and began to cry, trying to crawl out of Mrs. Shott's arms and back into mine. I comforted her, saying I would see her again soon. Mrs. Shott instructed her to tell me how much she loved me, which made me want to laugh or cry or vomit, I wasn't sure which. When Karen was again smiling and saying, "See you later," I left.

September 11

For two days I wondered what to do next. I felt that if the Center deigned to give its permission, I still would not be able to work with Mrs. Shott. I will not compete for Karen's affection, as Mrs. Shott seems willing to do, nor can I give up my independence in my actions with Karen. On the other hand, as it stands, I am not able to see Karen alone, which is so valuable.

I was garnering my courage to call Mrs. Ling and explain everything to her and ask for permission to spend a few hours with Karen once a week at her house after school, with the baby-sitter but not the parents present, when Mrs. Ling called me herself. Mrs. Shott must have had the afterthought that I might report our meeting to Mrs. Ling and wanted a chance to tell her side of the story, because she called Mrs. Ling. She told her she wants Karen to identify school solely with her: "When Karen thinks of school, I want her to think of Mrs. Shott." (She seems to refer to herself always in the third person.) Therefore, she does not think it beneficial that I start coming to the Center right away; she will call me or Mrs. Ling in about a month, or when she feels the proper time has come. Mrs. Ling had wanted to start visiting the class regularly herself on her mornings off from work, but Mrs. Shott told her she had better call first to ask for an appointment so she wouldn't interfere with her class.

Mrs. Ling mentioned at this point that she at least intends to attend PTA meetings this year, which she did not do too often last year. Perhaps, she said, she would make a request that only foster grandmothers who actually *like* children be hired.

Mrs. Ling anticipated my reaction to Mrs. Shott, since it was basically the same as hers, which saved me from having to do a lot of explaining. Relieved, I made my suggestion that I see Karen at her house when she comes home from school. Before I could say anything about my discontent over not being able to see Karen alone, Mrs. Ling, to my grateful surprise, brought up the subject. She had noticed how I had to run from one of them to the other, trying not to seem impolite to either; why didn't she start bringing Karen over for an hour or so to visit me by herself on Friday nights? She could then stay and visit when she came to pick Karen up. Naturally, I agreed.

Because of Mrs. Ling's understanding, I can avoid Mrs. Shott and still see Karen alone. I was also very much pleased that Mrs. Ling felt it unnecessary that I should work with Karen according to Mrs. Shott's dictates, since, in her words, "You are like a mother to her; you provide companionship and love."

September 13 and 20

So far Karen and I have had two successive Friday evenings alone together. During the first evening, although Mrs. Ling was not physically present, her shadow certainly was manifest. Karen continually repeated her mother's commands: "Sha-lai!

Don't play piggyback! Get down! Shush! Don't tell me to shush!" ad nauseam. My impulse was to tell her to shut up (another command!), but I realized that it will take her a few such hours alone before we can reestablish our free-floating relationship.

Karen was keyed up during the first visit, running from bathroom to bedroom to kitchen, where she dragged the milk carton from the refrigerator and demanded numerous refills of her cup.

She also played a long time with the telephone (a toy one is a big favorite with the Ling children), dialing and saying "hello, hello, hello." I have never heard her say "hello" to anyone directly, but she will say "hi" if pressed.

When John called from work, I let her talk to him. She said "Hello, hello, hello," and then tried her best to hang up the receiver. I finally regained possession of it, but then was commanded by her to "Put the telephone away!"

By the second visit, she seemed to know the new visiting procedure and danced around the apartment for the first few, excited moments, telling me with a big grin, "We don't *have* to say bye-bye!"

The bathroom continues to fascinate her. She made pee twice, unrolling vast amounts of toilet paper and stuffing it, quite unused, down the toilet. I had to retrieve as much as I could, to her displeasure. "Flush it!" she commanded and steered my hand to the lever. "You flush it" was my response. "*You* flush it!" came back the angry words until I finally did flush it.

Actually, we argued quite a bit in the bathroom tonight. She gave me commands in faulty language, but because she was directing my hand toward the task, her meaning was clear. For example, she turned on the sink faucets and played with the water. Being unable to turn them back off, she put my hand on the faucet and said, "Turn the water on!" I refused, saying, "It is on, Karen." She repeated her request several times, growing more and more angry and frustrated, until finally she said, "Turn the water *off*!" We went through the same conflict over the light switch. Whether she really does not know the difference between on and off, or whether she is simply too lazy or stubborn with her word usage, I do not know.

While Karen got away a little bit from repeating her mother's specific commands about our play together, her overall speech consisted of sentences other people direct at her. "Don't play!" "Don't hit the TV!" "Don't grind your teeth!"

We spent almost two hours together and toward the end we were both tired and subdued. For a good half hour, Karen sat on the couch and twiddled with a string on her jacket and an empty envelope, once moving closer to the small television next to the couch so she could watch her twiddling reflection.

She chanted to herself all the while, different short sentences, the sounds of which she soon modified so much that they became unintelligible. "Don't play with your fingers" soon became "don't pl . . ." and finally "do–pl." "Give me a kiss" and several other phrases received the same treatment.

Karen seemed to twiddle almost with desperation; probably neither her mother nor Mrs. Shott indulges this activity too much anymore. Her withdrawal was not as complete as during the first few months, at least; she let me know, with big smiles every once in a while, that she was still aware of my presence, and she leaned against my leg as I rubbed her back.

September 27

After this visit, I am more worried about Karen than I have allowed myself to be in a long time. For almost the whole hour, she repeated, "Don't you make that noise. Karen, Karen, Karen, don't you make that noise!" At one point, watching her as she sat in a corner of the couch munching on potato chips and repeating this sentence in all its variations and sound modifications, I could not help but think that anyone seeing her now would consider her not much more than a babbling idiot.

She has also regressed to some bizarre posturing, which I thought she had long ago given up. She held a potato chip in her hand and circumscribed circles with it, one jerky movement per circle. Then she bent forward at the waist, so that the top half of her body was almost parallel with the floor, and repeated several more jerky circles.

Later this week, I dreamed that Karen was hit by a car, or rather when I saw her she was sitting between a car's front wheels, so I assumed she had been hit. She told me she wasn't sure I would come, and I assured her that of course, I will always come to her. When I awoke, I felt as if this dream were a reproach to me. Karen was being "hit" by something big, and I was not doing enough to help her.

I resolved to start by talking with Mrs. Ling about Karen's echoing all the commands she receives. If Mrs. Ling could only hear herself talk, she would see that almost every sentence she utters to her daughter is a command. I am sure this is doubly true in school, what with Mrs. Shott's commander-like attitude.

October 4

As soon as I opened my door tonight, Karen ran in, threw off her jacket, and began to dance in spinning circles. I was glad to see that she still looks forward to our time together.

Before Mrs. Ling left, I tentatively tried to keep my promise to myself. First I asked whether she had spoken with Mrs. Shott recently about Karen's progress. Well, no, because Mrs. Shott did not schedule the first parent conference until November, which we both agreed was a time ridiculously late into the semester.

I proceeded further to ask if Mrs. Ling herself has seen improvement in Karen. Her answer was so overwhelmingly positive that I cowardly abandoned my resolve to bring out my own misgivings. It seems Karen is reaching out toward her baby brother Theodore as a playmate, which would indeed be a tremendous boost for her social development. Mrs. Ling said that a few days ago, for example, Karen was lying on her bed, wedged in the space between the mattress and the wall, and she called out to Theodore who was also lying on the bed: "Come, Theodore, come in the corner."

Mrs. Ling added that because she continues to

be aware of substantial progress, she is reluctant to take Karen for another psychological examination. As she left, she said to Karen, "Come give Mommy a kiss!" Karen came across the room to stand on tiptoe and give her mother a puckered kiss on the lips. "See? Last year she wouldn't do that!" (Note: I have learned that in traditional Chinese culture, parents rarely kiss their children, expressing affection instead by a pat on the head. So while it had seemed strange to me that Mrs. Ling never used to kiss Karen, actually it was not strange at all.)

I was to feel relieved, temporarily, that I had kept my peace, for tonight Karen proved an absolute charm. She munched on crackers, danced, used the toilet a few times, answered the ringing telephone with "Hello John" and proceeded to tell him, "Don't be lazy!" over and over again. However, this conversation with John was the only time she got hung up on a command.

She did not lose herself in twiddling, either; in fact, the few times I thought she was on the verge of doing so, she resolutely put the paper or magazine down after a second or two and turned to me with a big grin. I could almost see her making the decision: no, I don't want to do that tonight. Time after time she clambered into my lap and tenderly played with my face and hair.

I could not believe the change in Karen from one Friday to the next. After the last visit, I was in despair; tonight I feel as if she's pulling through. I do think her time with me (and with John also, for the few minutes they spend together after he comes home from work) is a valuable release for her.

October 6

Today, Sunday, we paid a social visit to the Ling family, which included a ride in the country and a delicious Chinese dinner. Although it was a visit with the whole family, a social occasion, I did make a few mental notes about Karen.

She is indeed more aware of Theodore than before. Mrs. Ling told me he follows Karen all around and imitates her play and speech. Aside from the obvious good it will do Karen for her to have an admiring, noncritical presence intruding upon consciousness, I realized today that perhaps her language will develop as Theodore's does. I noticed during our car ride, for example, that when someone would say "Look at that house," both Karen and Theodore would repeat "house."

I also noticed that one of Karen's paintings from school is now taped up on the wall, and a frame of photos in the family room, formerly only of Tommy, now includes one of Karen.

Karen was much quieter here than at my apartment, and if not being directly paid attention to, immediately lapsed into solitary playing and twiddling. Her parents, however, seemed less demanding of her than I have noticed in the past and gave her far fewer commands. All in all, Karen's life seems on the upswing again.

October 11

We finally made some progress tonight with Karen's bathroom fixation. Each visit she spends a total of ten to fifteen minutes running into the bathroom, turning on the light, pretending to make pee, putting reams of toilet paper in the bowl, screaming "*You* flush it!" as she turns off the lights, and then running in fright from the noise of the flush. Tonight, however, we spent perhaps twice as much time as usual in the bathroom. No sooner would she run out than she would run back in.

The first sign of progress I noticed was her correct usage of "on" and "off," after I thought my weekly attempts to teach her were going for naught. ("On, Karen, o–n, on! The light *is* off, turn it on!") Tonight she said "Turn the light on," and after she had turned it on, she repeated the words of praise I had not even been aware that I use, till that moment: "That's a girl!" Next, she helped me to flush the toilet several times and then finally did it all by herself.

I was wondering where all these bathroom trips were going to lead when Karen, after sitting on the toilet for a few pensive moments, jumped up, turned around, squeezed her crotch together and leaned over the bowl, managing to spray out a few drops. Then she spent more time than usual tucking in her shirt and arranging the front of her pants. At last I realized that she was imitating the actions of a man at the toilet.

She went through these motions several more times during the next few minutes, while I talked to her about how women are different than men, how we sit down to pee, how brother Tommy has a penis, and so forth. She seemed to be paying attention, and repeated "penis" after I said it. She began craning her neck around to look at her bare bottom, which had sores near her rectum as usual (I have never discovered why). I patted it and admired it, wondering whether she was looking for a penis back there!

October 25

We had to skip a week because Mrs. Ling had an activity to attend at her school. When I opened my door tonight, Karen ran immediately into the bathroom, shouting "Take off your pants! Take off your pants!" while her mother watched in disapproval. Karen is certainly not yet capable of discretion. It worries me that if Mrs. Ling pictures her daughter spending the evening in my bathroom every week, she may withdraw her enthusiasm from this project.

After Mrs. Ling left, Karen spent some time playing with the toilet, but not as much as last time. She did, at one point, again stand against the bowl, spread her crotch with her fingers, and take a pee in this fashion. She didn't seem quite so fixated about it this week, and I offered no commentary but merely watched.

One of the things that Karen plays with during our visits is a picture of a naked African woman and child who are sitting together on a log. I have it pasted on a piece of cardboard about the size of a postcard, and Karen frequently carries it around the apartment with her. Although I talk to her about the picture, she had never responded verbally and had often laid it face down on the couch or floor.

Tonight, however, the picture happened to be missing from its usual spot. I had propped it on some high shelves, out of Karen's direct sight. She noticed it was missing, and several times said "A woman, a woman" before I realized her meaning and fetched it for her. She looked at it intently, pointing to the "woman" as she said the word, then the baby's "tummy," and finally back to the woman's "breast." I think this picture holds special appeal for her because it shows such harmony between naked mother and naked baby.

She is again seeing the speech therapist for a half hour daily, and her speech is immediately affected, as she practices and plays with words on her own initiative. While eating a cracker, for example, she played verbally with "cracker, crap, cramp." I added "crumb, cracker crumb" to spruce up her repertoire.

We also sang and she was quite affectionate, frequently running to my lap and giving me hard hugs. Her hugs consist of putting her cheek next to mine and then pushing with all her might against it.

November 1

This was one of the very few sessions which I have canceled. I had a rotten day, preceded by a rotten week. I was dead tired and in a foul mood. I knew I would not be able to respond to Karen at all, and of course I suffered mighty guilt pangs.

November 8

Karen arrived missing one front tooth and looking altogether different because of it. Her mother said Karen had been very upset when it became loose and often came to have her touch it. When the tooth did at last fall out, there was some blood which further frightened Karen. Mrs. Ling commented that she was pleased Karen knew enough to come to her when she was troubled.

I realize more and more how entangled this whole problem is: Karen's actions usually make Mrs. Ling feel inadequate as a mother and her resulting hurt feelings then rebound upon Karen.

It has become part of our bathroom ritual for her to invite me to use the toilet. Although she sometimes closes her eyes and turns coyly away, a word from me is enough for her to approach and see that my anatomy is the same as hers. Often she leans on my back while I am sitting there.

November 22

We have again gone two weeks without seeing each other. Mrs. Ling had another school activity last week. She wondered if we should even stop these visits because of my advancing pregnancy, or perhaps she should stay for the hour to keep Karen from crawling over me. I assured her that I wanted to continue the visits as long as possible and that Karen was not too rough.

Tonight Karen was very, very happy to see me. I could easily initiate her coming to hug me, laughing in delight, by saying one of our "call words": washing machine, M–M, or hmm–hmm–hmm (hummed liltingly). We again spent most of our time in the bathroom which tends, unfortunately, to make me irritable. I keep telling myself how important it is for Karen.

While looking in the bathroom mirror, she named her nose and teeth (her other front one is loose now) and then, touching them said, "Breasts. These are breasts." I suggested she get the picture of the woman and baby. She immediately ran into the living room and searched for it. I found it for her, and she touched and identified the baby's breasts and tummy and the woman's breasts.

By our hour's end, she had found a ballpoint pen on the floor and spent the remaining time twiddling it before her face. Her mother and brother Tommy came to pick her up, and while I was talking with them, Karen wandered around the living room, slapping her hands and face. Mrs. Ling ignored her, but I went over to hug her so I could unobtrusively stop her slaps.

As they were leaving, Karen reached out for Tommy's hand to get him to hurry. Once her evening with me is over, she doesn't like to waste time over good-byes.

November 28

Thanksgiving Day. We were invited to eat dinner with the Lings. Again, since it was a social occasion I had little opportunity to be with Karen alone. During the few minutes which we did have, she climbed into her baby brother's high chair, taking her "lit–tle ted–dy bear" with her, and made me secure the tray for her. Then the game began of her throwing the bear down on the floor, with me retrieving it and "attacking" her as I returned it. She screamed with laughter.

I also watched her with her Dr. Seuss alphabet book, which elicited some painful memory pangs from me as I saw her recite letters, words, and phrases which I had taught her what seems like many months ago.

Mrs. Ling mentioned that there is someone working with Karen this semester at the Center, a girl Mrs. Ling knows personally from her school. It is good that Mrs. Shott finally surrendered to the fact that she needs some help, but I cannot help feeling envious since I had been the first to volunteer my services for working with Karen there this semester. At any rate, Mrs. Ling said the girl is able to eat lunch with Karen and that she has "forced" Karen to eat the various lunches the school provides, which eliminates the need for Mrs. Ling to pack a lunch for her each day.

Karen was limping slightly today. Apparently she had been jumping on the trampoline unattended the day before at school and had fallen, bruising her ankle. No one noticed until Karen was putting on her socks at the end of the day, when Mrs. Shott saw that her ankle was so swollen that she at first thought Karen had stuffed something into her sock besides her foot. They took her to the hospital and summoned Mrs. Ling, who said Karen howled in fear while being X-rayed. There were no broken bones, and Karen ripped off the bandages as soon as she got home. Mrs. Ling said she shuddered to think of the problems had there been a broken bone and Karen had had to wear a cast. Mr. Ling said he gave the people at school a talking-to for their inattentiveness. I, too, am surprised that they allow Karen to use the trampoline by herself, but I know how much she loves to jump and how elusive she can be.

Mostly today I became more aware of Karen's relationship with her father and brother Tommy. During dinner she kept jumping up from the table and running around to give Tommy a smack. Then she would return to her seat, looking worried and saying "Don't hit!" Mr. Ling urged Tommy to hit her back, which finally resulted in Tommy's bouncing around in front of Karen, egging her to come on and fight. Mr. Ling himself even made a fist (and a huge fist it is) and held it at Karen's chin, saying "See this?" in a threatening tone.

Mrs. Ling told me they disagree on how to react to Karen's hitting Tommy, because she herself feels it is best to ignore her. I have always seen that Mr. Ling shows no tenderness toward Karen, but tonight I saw the strict disciplinarian side of his attitude toward her.

December 6 and 11

I had to cancel two weeks in a row because I had the flu.

December 20

As always, when Karen hasn't been here for a while, she spent a lot of time repeating commands until she relaxed. That's one reason I so hate to skip our evenings. Tonight she spent the time mostly in the bathroom either on the toilet or on a chair looking at herself in the mirror. She would rather have me lift her up and hold her while she looks, but I am much too pregnant and she has accepted a chair as substitute, provided I keep an arm around her.

We shared an unusually pleasant moment as she sat on the toilet and I sat on the edge of the bathtub across from her. I held and stroked her hand, and she not only did not withdraw her hand, but also allowed intense, close-range eye contact for almost a minute.

We also sang as we sat there: "Doe, a deer, a female deer." Karen surprised me by singing quite a few of the lines all by herself in a stream, probably the most words I have heard her utter at one time. I noticed her pronunciation is improving. She does tend to slur, especially when she sings unfamiliar words, so I carefully enunciate all the words when we sing together.

December 27

I again had to cancel because of illness. Karen and Mrs. Ling stopped by briefly during the week to deliver Christmas presents. Karen immediately threw off her coat and shoes and ran to the refrigerator to see what was available.

December 31

New Year's Eve. We went to the Ling's for dinner. Karen greeted me as I entered the house by pulling down her pants and showing me her bare bottom. I looked away, pretending not to notice so she wouldn't get into trouble; her mother quickly dragged her off to the toilet.

Karen is on vacation from school, and Mrs. Ling says she has been letting her stay up later than usual so that they can have time together in private. Karen loves to sit with her and draw and write; Mrs. Ling is trying to teach her to connect her phrases into complete sentences.

That she is succeeding in this endeavor was proved to me when Mr. Ling announced "bedtime" in a stern voice. Karen gave him a dark, withering look; she and I were having a very pleasant time drawing together. Instead of answering him directly, she ordered me to print: "Stay here. Karen stay here."

January 3

The Lings are afraid I am getting too big to cope with Karen, but I want to continue as long as possible, so we started off the New Year right by having a regular visit. As soon as they arrived, Karen ran into the bathroom. Mrs. Ling scolded her in a superharsh voice, telling her to get out of there. The admonition retained its force even after Mrs. Ling had gone, so Karen and I drew pictures in the living room. Karen sublimated her urges by having me draw a "potty," then a "flush-it," which she flushed with her fingernail: "boom!"

When she did return to the bathroom, she alternated between the mirror and the toilet, managing two or three bowel movements in the process. After each one, she turned to inspect her production, blowing and poking it with toilet paper until it sank to the bowl's bottom. I am trying to teach her to wipe herself, and in the appropriate place at the appropriate time, but it is a slow process.

When she brings her cup for me to fill with milk, I say, "Tell me, Karen, don't show me. *Tell me* what you want," until she responds with "I want a drink of milk." She is improving every week. At her house last week, Mrs. Ling was surprised when Karen said "I want to get down" when she wanted to get out of the high chair and I made her tell me so, instead of showing me.

"Karen, you said the right thing!" Mrs. Ling exclaimed.

Again, by the end of our time together Karen had found two ballpoint pens and was twiddling them, like a conductor with dual batons, in front of the mirror. She did interrupt herself several times, however, to turn and give me big hugs and smiles, so I knew she wasn't completely out of touch with reality.

‡‡

This entry was to be the final one, marking the last private time that Karen and I shared. Almost a year to the day after I first went to the Special Education Center, Mrs. Ling called to tell me she did not want to burden me during the last months of my pregnancy. Try as I might, I couldn't change her mind.

Our son was born that March; in July we moved to another state. During our farewell visit to the Lings, Karen's speech had noticeably regressed during the six months since I had last seen her. It was again full of grunts and heavy breathing. When I had to turn my attention away from her and toward my baby, she would begin hitting herself in the face with whatever toy she was holding.

Mrs. Ling told me a psychiatrist had observed Karen in school and judged that Karen was quite intelligent and not retarded, but that she would indeed be considered retarded in a few years, if unimproved. She would fall too far behind her age group to be able to catch up. The psychiatrist's advice was to treat Karen as a two-year-old, acceding as far as possible to her every wish.

From what I could see, Mrs. Ling was not following this advice, at least not during our visit. For example, Mr. Ling cut into a large watermelon, and both he and Mrs. Ling commanded Karen to open her mouth and receive chunks from their forks. Karen held each piece in her mouth, eyes watering, for a few minutes before either swallowing it or secretly spitting it out on my husband's plate. Mrs. Ling remarked that while strawberries and melons were her own favorite fruits, Karen hated them and so had to be fed them in this way.

How to summarize the relationship Karen and I had? Something Bettelheim wrote keeps coming to mind, that when a psychotic child begins to laugh, the psychosis has become more benign. When she called to tell me she would no longer be bringing Karen over, Mrs. Ling herself reminded me that Karen was mostly expressionless a year ago, while now she smiles and laughs. I regard this as my sole undisputed accomplishment with Karen: our relationship has made her disturbance more benign.

II. The Group Home

Working in a group home for autistic children as a behavioral technician was, as I suggested in the introduction, strikingly different from working as a volunteer with Karen. For one thing, all six boys were at least five years older than Karen was when I met her; none of them was hypoactive, as she was, but all were more or less hyperactive, and much higher functioning as well.

Another major difference had to do with the theoretical orientation, because by now the overwhelming consensus of the professional community was that autism *is* a developmental disability; it *is* an organic dysfunction. The issue was not presented to us as arguable. What continues to be debatable, because still unknown, is not only the cause (or causes) of autism, but also the precise nature of the defect. Although researchers presume the defect is somewhere in the central nervous system, arguments have been variously advanced for autism being a language deficit; a problem of perceptual inconstancy; a central cognitive defect; a cross-modal association defect; a problem caused by lack of cerebral dominance; a result of cerebral asymmetries and temporal lobe damage. None of these high-sounding theories—and there are more than these—

has, in fact, generated any therapies of note, let alone cures. People who work with autistic children every day, especially in a nonacademic environment, do not usually keep track of the arguments since, rightly or no, they do not seem relevant.

More practical arguments for hands-on workers center on control of the child's behavior. Although institutionalized autistics are often medicated for their aggression and hyperactivity, the group-home residents were not, so we all tried hard to get the boys under what we called "verbal control." We also used the methods found most successful in teaching autistic children, those of behavior modification. Although initially I had reservations about the techniques of behaviorism, I had, by 1980, little or no choice if I wanted to work with this population. I have learned since to respect behaviorism for how it can help a child change his own behavior and allow him to learn. Moreover, food was not used in the group home as a reinforcer, contrary to the stereotype of bribing children to be "good" with M&Ms. The preferred choice was to use "natural consequences" as reinforcers, although this could not always be carried out in practice. I must admit, however, that I always derived keen pleasure from watching a child, following an inner dictate clearly more powerful than what had been written into his program, develop a passionate hatred for his carefully chosen reinforcers, one after the other. The only predictable aspect of autistic children's behavior is their unpredictability. One has to admire that.

I suppose the dispiriting part of this new medical

dogma, although we were told it corresponded more closely with reality than the old, was the death of the rescue fantasy. No one expected, ever, for any of the boys to be cured, or normal, or non-autistic; the hope was, for the highest functioning, that they might earn their livings in sheltered workshops and perhaps live in less supervised facilities; for the lowest functioning, the future continues to lie in group homes, which is a far better future than autistic children have had in the past. A few years ago, no one ever heard of autistic *adults*, because when the children reached the age of eighteen or twenty-one they were usually reclassified as mentally retarded and put into institutions, where often they did not survive for long.

Although we knew the boys could, and certainly did, make progress, and although we derived satisfaction from each increment, no matter how small, still the perceived futility could be wearing. This job demanded extraordinary amounts of energy and patience; it was sometimes difficult to sustain enthusiasm and a flow of fresh ideas for helping the boys. Even though most of the staff vehemently protested against the possibility of becoming "burnt out," I think none of us was immune. The potential for physical abuse, and what is in a sense more terrifying, psychological abuse, is undeniably present. These issues will need to be addressed as group homes become more and more prevalent; I raise them here because at the moment they seem largely ignored.

The group home was the brainchild of the boys' families. Although the decision for such a placement must have been agonizing for many of the parents, still the presence of an autistic child in a family can be ongoing agony, both for the marriage relationship and for the other, normal children. And there is truly no way a family can provide the same attention as a facility with twenty-four-hour staff.

The boys lived seven days a week in the group home; they attended autistic classrooms in a public school, going back and forth by bus. Their time before and after school was extremely structured, at least in theory, for autistic children respond best to a structured environment. This took the form of household chores, since the boys were being taught as many living skills as possible, and community outings, to teach the boys how to function and the community how to react. I say "in theory," because in reality it is extremely difficult to structure every minute of *anyone's* time. One argument ran that since the group home was supposed to duplicate a normal living experience, then free time should be part of that normalcy. But of course, autistic children do not know how to use free time "appropriately" (a big word in the group home), so this argument led to the, in my opinion, lunacy of installing a giant color television set in the living room. The boys sat and stimmed, while the staff watched their favorite shows. In all fairness, however, the issue of how to spend free time with autistic children is a tricky one, one assuredly in need of new and creative approaches.

It is important to keep in mind that during the span of the three months or so which this journal covers, I had been converted to the new faith, the new dogma of autism. I was sure I was working with brain-damaged children, although I did prefer to think that their brains were processing differently, rather than incorrectly. Still, the problem was of the brain, not the psyche. Of course, psychic material has crept into my accounts, because that is of greater interest to me than, for example, seizures, but the change in style and content from the diary of my work with Karen is evident.

While my entries deal mostly with *my* work with the boys, obviously I was not the only staff member, and by no means was I even a particularly important one. I have focused on my work because I know it best, because (as with Karen) I thought a journal would help me keep track of problems and progress, and also, frankly, because recording all the staff transactions with each other and the boys would have been a formidable task. The group home had an administrative director, but the day-to-day operation was run by the house manager; next in line were the two houseparents, who worked alternately, not together, and last of all came the behavioral technicians, full and part time. Eventually a strict staff-to-child ratio of 1:2 was enforced, but in the early days one houseparent and one technician frequently were in charge of all six boys. Although literally we on the bottom were expected to take orders from everyone above us, in reality we worked more as a team, especially in the beginning months. At weekly staff meetings, for example, everyone's input was encouraged and together we made decisions about the boys.

Finding qualified, compassionate workers for the home proved to be an ongoing problem, however, especially for the less desirable shifts. Turnover became too high. As group homes prove themselves an attractive alternative to institutions, thorough staff training and decent salaries will be necessary, plus ways in which to keep morale and dedication high. My personal view is that hands-on workers with autistic children, while perhaps not as professionally sophisticated as others in the mental health field, have much to offer in terms of practical understanding and treatment. One problem is that they do not really have a forum for their ideas; the other, obvious but overlooked, is that people who work with autistic children get very *tired.* I am sure many bright ideas have drifted away in a fog of fatigue before they can even be expressed.

What I have, in any case, tried to capture in the pages that follow are snapshots, imperfectly composed and focused, yet genuine, of life in an autistic group home.

‡‡

Thursday

I don't usually work during the week, but today I was asked to come in because the boys were being excused from school to attend a city-sponsored picnic, complete with rock band, puppet show, and free hot dogs.

Someone at the staff meeting yesterday had complained about their missing school. Lucy, the house manager, explained that such an outing, accessible to *all* children, would be a "good, normalizing experience" for ours. Group homes are big on "normalizing experiences"; they comprise one major raison d'être. Handicapped people should be helped to be as normal and as independently functioning as possible. For autistic kids, this means being able to go out into the community, however crowded or noisy the event, without tantrumming, pulling a stranger's hair, or (as James once did), trying to take a bottle away from a baby in its mother's arms. It's not easy.

Bruce would not be going. He was scheduled to go to the hospital for an EEG. On the previous attempt, he failed to fall asleep, which is necessary for the test, so this time he will be given a strong muscle relaxant.

I was late arriving; two of the other staff had already gone to pick up the boys from school. I waited outside. It was a hot day. In a few minutes, before I even saw the car, I recognized Mack's screaming. There he was, tantrumming away in the back seat. By the time I got there, Otis (a brand new houseparent) had opened the back door and Mack now lay on his back on the sidewalk, kicking and screaming, "No go in the car!"

I tried to calm him down. He rewarded my efforts with a mouthful of spit. Then he banged his head back, hard, on the concrete. At this point Otis picked him up, arms under his armpits, and marched him across the street and into the house.

Mack is eight years old, tall for his age, with beautiful red hair, clear skin and freckles. I sat with him on the couch and patiently explained to him what we would be doing, in sequence, over and over.

"It'll be a nice picnic, Mack."

"Go on a picnic. Eat hot dog."

"Yes! Hot dogs. And there'll be music, too."

"Moo–nik."

"And I came today especially to go to the picnic with you, Mack."

"Go on a pic–nic with Mack."

"Okay."

I took him upstairs so he could change into shorts. On the way I asked Otis, "Did anyone think to tell Mack this morning when he left for school that he was leaving early for a picnic?"

"No, I don't think anyone mentioned it."

"You really have to prepare him for schedule changes. Disruptions in routine set him off."

"Well, he'll just have to get used to it, won't he."

Otis had just come from being a houseparent in a well-established group home in another state, and felt more than a little superior to the rest of us. And well he might, at least in terms of experience, since I was the only one who had ever worked with an autistic child before; none of us had ever even worked in a group home. Yet I think we all had one big advantage over Otis; we truly loved the boys and felt between us a special spirit, born of the fact that we had worked together to get the home opened up and together had welcomed the boys, one by one, to live there. We were less willing than Otis, I suppose, merely to "force" the boys to act normally. We saw each boy as a unique personality, each with his own special emotional needs.

It was true that the most classic characteristic Mack brought to the home was his resistance to change, especially changes in motion. On a walk, he would throw a tantrum if made to turn a corner; he just wanted to keep on forever in the same straight direction. An uninformed driver was in for a surprise at the first turn, or even the first red light. "No stop! No stop!"

The park was a hot, noisy mob scene, but the boys did very well, except for Lincoln, our eleven-year-old, who twice left the group and had to be tracked down. One of the ultimate nightmares of working here: losing a kid.

By the time we got back to the house, Bruce had returned from the hospital and was sound asleep from the effects of the drug. He was breathing so very shallowly I was not sure he was breathing at all, so I shook him a little. A minute later he woke up enough to stumble into the bathroom. He looked absolutely frightful, his normally pale complexion pure chalk, punctuated by black eyes. He fell back asleep on the toilet, without ever urinating. The doctors said he probably wouldn't eat or drink for a half a day, either, because his throat muscles would be too relaxed.

Later, I went upstairs by myself to use the bathroom before going home. As I closed the door behind me, the doorknob fell off. I couldn't get it back on; I was locked in. I screamed out the window for five long minutes before someone downstairs heard and came to the rescue. Undoubtedly the neighbors heard me, too, but figured I was just another crazy kid.

Saturday

The beginning of the weekend: my regularly scheduled work shift. I arrived around 6:00 A.M.

The "awake person" was busily reading his school books. The awake person is so named because he or she has to stay awake all night and keep alert for trouble. Autistic children are infamous for their sleep disturbances. The other major duty is to toilet, as we say, the three younger boys—James, Mack, and Bruce—two or three times in hopes of avoiding wet sheets. Some nights are drier than others, but an *all* dry night is a rare event.

Mack was the only child up, and his roommate Sylvester had gone home for a few days, so I took him downstairs. It was pleasant to work with just one child in the morning stillness of the big house. I made a pot of coffee while he unloaded the dishwasher, telling me all the while the day's schedule: "Unload dishwasher. Then get dressed. Make-a bed. Eat breakfast. Do work. Then after lunch, go on a train ride."

"You got it, Mack. You got it."

Mack did a perfect job of unloading and putting away the dishes. Twas not ever thus. When he first came to the group home, his mother had said that she loved her "sugar baby" very much, but it was becoming impossible to live with him anymore. She mentioned something cryptically about having a Rubbermaid house. We quickly found out what she meant: within a week he had broken every lamp and was working on the kitchen glass supply. He was not at all sneaky about it; in fact, he would always warn us: "Mack go upstairs, throw paint." Then he would run upstairs, grab a jar of red paint, and hurl it against the wall. The staff could never ever let him out of sight, not even for a second.

After a glass of milk at dinner, Mack would announce, "Mack break glass." Sometimes you could stop him, sometimes not. He greeted the shattered pieces with shrieks of joyous laughter; being made to clean up after himself was like frosting on the cake. Eventually we smartened up and bought plastic cups. The lamps remained in a perpetually patched together state.

The morning was indeed spent doing work, and also charting it. Every boy has a clipboard filled with charts of household tasks (vacuuming, sweeping, doing laundry) as well as personal skills (dressing, toileting, hair brushing) which are broken down into many steps. We mark down how independently he does each step, and also how much time the whole process takes. Mack, for example, dresses pretty well independently, but it might take him forty-five minutes to do it. Today it took that long because he kept shouting "Zucchini *off* pretzel" and "You do *not* take off Daddy's diaper" and suchlike.

I charted Mack's dressing, bedmaking, and washing his clothes. Next I worked with Bruce for a while, charting his handwashing and hairbrushing. Bruce is very "prompt-dependent," which means he can stand in front of the sink seemingly forever until someone tells him to turn the water on and continues to guide him through, step by step.

This is common in autistic children; also common are the times they whirl through the process without being prompted at all. This random independence can strain your credulity, let alone your patience, during the do-nothing times: Is the child being stubborn? Manipulative? Has he forgotten the sequence this time? Or does his brain see it as a different, as yet unlearned, sequence, because the soap dish is on the left side of the faucet this time instead of the right? We don't know.

This morning Bruce wants to stroke the insides of his wrists with his fingertips and kiss his palm while rubbing his nose instead of washing his hands. Then he threw his hairbrush on the floor and ran out of the bathroom screaming. As I fetched him back, he grabbed hold of my hair and yanked, hard, laughing as he did so.

Bruce often has seemed the most unreachable boy in many ways. A tall and thin nine-year-old with strawberry blond hair, he seems to pop continually in and out of focus, which makes working with him frustrating. The first time I met him, I was struck by what a fearful child he seemed. He was saying good-bye to his mother, tearfully, tentatively plucking at her clothes, standing on tiptoe. Of all the boys, he reminded me most of Karen because of this apparent fear. In the beginning, too, he was the most physically quiet. If everyone else was tantrumming, you could count on Bruce to sit peaceably on the couch and wait for someone to attend to him.

The honeymoon didn't last long, though, either because he figured being quiet didn't garner him much attention (our mistake) or because he could no longer withstand the noise pressure of his surroundings. He became a screamer and a climber, becoming so active that he acquired a hip infection from the constant flexing movement.

He brought to the home very little speech that

was not echolalic, either immediate or delayed. Delayed echolalia means the child suddenly repeats sentences or even whole conversations heard sometime in the past. Thus, for example, we were made privy to parental arguments, complete with inflection—"You son of a *beech*"—and vigorous gesturing.

I also set Lincoln to work on one of his jobs—cleaning the kitchen cabinet doors. He has thirty minutes in which to finish. If he makes it, he can have five minutes of looking at Lawn-Boy brochures. He gets done in twenty-nine minutes, so I give him the ads. That, in essence, is his behavior program.

The afternoon's outing was changed from a train ride to a car ride, much to Mack's chagrin, although thankfully he didn't tantrum. My shift was supposed to end as they left. At the last moment, when I was washing pots and pans from lunch, Susie came back into the house with Rod, saying he had somehow gotten the bottom drawstrings of his jacket wound around his penis.

Rod is fifteen years old, but you would never guess it to look at him: he is very small for his age. He tends to hunch when he walks, holding his arms slightly behind his body, and tiptoe, unless you remind him to get down on his heels. He speaks only a few words, and those poorly, although he loves to imitate sounds; he didn't talk at all until a couple of years ago. This lack of speech was the symptom that alerted his parents. Otherwise he was a cuddly, responsive baby who later amazed his family with his ability to keep five or six saucepan lids spinning at the same time.

Rod is an orderly person—closing doors, shutting drawers, taking a full coffee cup out of your hands to dump it in the sink. He's a ham as well. He stuffs all sorts of household wares under his shirt, or tries to hang them on his ears to make you laugh. He finds burps and sneezes very amusing; he also derives excruciating pleasure from producing streams of nasal mucus, particularly at the dinner table.

That's when he is in a good mood; when he has a tantrum, which is a mild-sounding term for his rages, he can be terrifying. His arms are scarred from self-inflicted bites. He can knock over heavy pieces of furniture like toothpicks. His mother told me she had no doubt Rod could bite someone's finger off. Because of these rages, Rod got his own personal behavioral therapist quite soon after coming to the home, to work with him on his behavior program. This consists of his working for stickers. In the beginning he stuck these all over his shirt and even ate special favorites; now he is more blasé and keeps them in a special notebook. When he earns a specified number of stickers, he cashes them in for a record or tape. He sits on the couch, rocking, rocking in rhythm, looking at the middle finger of his left hand (a visual stim), with a huge grin on his face. His current favorite is Janis Ian, but he likes Crystal Gayle and Fleetwood Mac, too.

Susie is his second therapist so far, and not terribly effective with him. Now she took him into the bathroom and I went out to tell everybody else, already loaded into two cars, the reason for the delay. It occurred to me to suggest to Dolores, the other houseparent, that Susie could probably use her help. Dolores is very good with Rod. She and I shared a chuckle over the unusual nature of the predicament, and then she hurried into the house. Susie met her at the door.

I could see their three bodies hurtling past the front window, plus James's father who happened to be there working on the house, for the next forty minutes or so. I had unwittingly sent Dolores into one of Rod's full-blown rages.

When she finally emerged, she was bleeding and her blouse had been torn. I felt incredibly guilty. Apparently, in trying to keep Susie from helping him, Rod had hit his head on a heavy cabinet door in the bathroom, shattering the mirror out of it onto the floor, all of which triggered a tantrum. Before the three adults could wrestle him down, he broke a lamp, knocked a huge bulletin board off the wall, spat and scratched. Once on the floor, he bit his own arms until they bled.

Sunday

A very peaceful day, which everybody found easy to take. Lincoln had gone home Saturday evening with his mother, and by 9:30 this morning James and Bruce had gone home for day visits. With Sylvester still away, that left only Mack and Rod.

Mack wasn't as happy about unloading the dishwasher as he was yesterday. Several times he hurled containers (thankfully, plastic) across the room and I made him sit down until he was calm again. Mack has a scream which rivals Bruce's in its piercing intensity.

Afterward, while cooking breakfast with Mack, I had to answer the phone. When I returned, he had turned the flame on under the frying pan, and had dipped two pieces of bread into the egg-and-milk batter before putting them in to cook. He had forgotten only to butter the pan. All right! That kid can really learn.

After breakfast I put him through his paces: dressing; stripping his bed; putting on clean sheets; washing the dirty ones; folding and putting away the clothes washed yesterday. That took us clear through to lunch. We packed sandwiches and fruit, and Mack and I, with Susie and Rod, went to the park to picnic and play.

For Mack, playing at the park means running. He likes to run along a border of some sort, hedges or a fence—in the house, he follows the baseboards—with a hand stiffly outstretched to touch it now and again. Sometimes he skips, but always it is back and forth, back and forth, today past a long row of hedges and up to the corner of the tennis court before turning back. I don't have to stay on top of him, just within calling distance, because sometimes he does break the ritual and forget to turn around.

One day a bona fide jogger happened to be running the same route as Mack. Each time they passed in opposite directions, Mack would put his arm out and lightly, every so lightly, touch the man's back. The jogger issued me several pained glances, but I pretended not to notice. He should be thankful, I decided, it was Mack and not James. James likes to lean over and smell people's butts.

Sylvester made the best comment on this not

very civilized habit: "But I didn't move into the group home to be smelled like a *rose*!"

Monday

Memorial Day. I worked the 2 to 10 P.M. shift. When I arrived, everyone was still at the park having a picnic lunch, so I walked up to meet them. A second after I spotted them, about one hundred yards off, I heard James screaming. Lucy was holding his feet and sponging his face, and Otis was holding his arms, trying to avoid his gouging fingernails. I relieved Otis while they told me the reason for the tantrum: they had told him to eat his sandwich before taking an apple and cookies for dessert. Lucy was in tears because he had butted his head backward into her nose. (Two weeks ago he had done the same move, fracturing the bone.)

He had repeatedly tried to bite Otis, who responded by putting his arm around James's neck and chin, leaving some nasty-looking marks in the process. Another nightmare of this job is that you will inadvertently injure a child while restraining him during a tantrum, or, frankly, that you will finally lose your professional patience and give him a good bash.

"Are you ready to eat your sandwich now, James?"

He nodded his head. We let him go. He sat up and took an open-handed swipe at Lucy. Back down he went. He screamed and tried to gouge my hands. We went on talking. After another few minutes, he got his hand free and made an indistinct sign.

"Are you ready to try it *now*, James?"

Again, a nod. But this time he sat up calmly, took the sandwich, chowed it right down, and never asked for dessert. We packed up and went home.

A typical James incident! This stubborn soul was eight years old when he moved into the group home. Although he can make a lot of noise and vocalize in super rhythm, he does not talk. Apparently he had a small vocabulary as a toddler, now lost. He has learned some sign language, but his education in this area was very haphazard, and many people in his environment do not even know how to sign. We have noticed that while in the presence of the several staff members who sign, his frequency of signing goes way up. Since he is a lazy signer at the best of times, it is as if he will not waste the energy on people who will not respond.

There is an ongoing argument, at the home and among autism workers in general, as to whether sign language should be taught at all to autistic children. The extreme "normalizing" faction argues that signing is normal only in the deaf community, where autistic people are not apt to be. The other side of the argument, whose side I take, is that these children need to communicate, in whatever normal or abnormal fashion happens to work the best. James, for example, is a child given to much bizarre behavior, such as feces-smearing and outrageous tantrums, like the one just described. Some of the tantrums, admittedly not all, have to be a consequence of his frustration at not being understood. Once I asked him what he wanted for breakfast; I misread his "pancake" sign for "sandwich." It took me ten minutes to calm him down.

In James's case, unfortunately, the argument is not resolved, so some of us sign to him and demand signing back; others do not actively encourage signing, but do respond, and still others haven't the slightest idea what his gestures mean. The upshot is that James has very few communication skills, at least expressively. His receptive vocabulary, which means words he understands when they are spoken, is impressively large. Anyone who disbelieves this need only discuss within his earshot a funny, clever, or nasty episode involving him and watch his joyous reaction. If possible, he even repeats the episode, as if to make you laugh all over again.

That morning, Rod had gone off again. Five people, including his mother, held him down for an hour and fifteen minutes. He hadn't done much material damage, but his poor arms were a mess. His mother cried briefly afterward and said, "Oh, to have to see my own son like this." Lucy said those words brought tears to all the staff's eyes. The other four boys were in the same room the whole time, because there was nobody available to take them elsewhere. At one point someone instructed Mack to go into the bathroom, get a towel, wet it, and bring it back. To everyone's surprise, he did it!

For about an hour I was alone in the backyard with James, Mack, and Lincoln. It was a very quiet time. Mack sat under a tree, digging holes with a stick and making piles of stones and leaves, not saying a word. Out of all the boys, he can play the most appropriately. Lincoln either rode his bike up and down the sidewalk or lay next to me in the grass, alternately sucking his thumb and asking about my vacuum cleaner(s) at home. "Do you have five? Why not?" James flapped big leaves or ran around, clapping his hands and kicking up his heels, or sat staring into the sunshine, munching dandelions. He also came to sit in my lap, pulling up his shirt for a rib scratch.

Later on, when we were a full crew again and barbecuing hamburgers, things got more hectic. Bruce did nothing but scream and attempt to climb over the high chain-link fence. James urinated on the sidewalk. Lincoln screamed at me because I wouldn't let him put the fifth gigantic spoonful of pickle relish on his miniscule hamburger. Mack moved his piles into the basement by inserting them, rock by rock, leaf by leaf, into the dryer vent on the side of the house.

Otis refused to let James eat his hamburger sandwich the way James would have preferred: take the meat out and eat the mustard-smeared bread. Consequently James didn't get too much; every time he tried to pick the sandwich apart, Otis or I removed his plate. He screamed and kicked a bit, but no real tantrum occurred. Actually he had snitched so much raw meat while helping Susie make the patties that he probably wasn't hungry enough to bother eating *our* way. James steals food whenever he has a chance, particularly honey, sugar, raw meat, and peanut butter, although once I caught him with a handful of uncooked rice. He is also, we discovered to our horror, fond of pink liquid medicines, like penicillin and Pepto-Bismol.

Later, while we were showering the boys, a neighbor came over to tell us a child was about to fall out of a window. It was Mack, laughing, about to go over. We grabbed him by the seat of his pants and dragged him in.

A few minutes later, I heard James screaming in the shower. He and Otis were certainly going through a power struggle these first few weeks of Otis's being here, a usual occurrence with a new staff member. James, especially, had to test the limits of any new person in the home. How much would he be able to get away with?

At last, everyone in bed! I sat in Bruce and James's room and sang a hopefully soporific song. It induced James to close his eyes, but Bruce kept yanking on my hair. If I moved too far away, he got out of bed and started stripping it down to the mattress. Finally I held his arms till he relaxed and got drowsy. By that time James was awake again. He snuck in Bruce's drawer and got a pajama top to flap in bed. That's illegal, but I pretended not to notice.

James's favorite stim is flapping a knotted sock or piece of hose or rolled up pajama piece. He holds the flapper in his right hand and sends it up to knock into his other palm, and then brings it back down mid-body to transcribe again a neat curve in space. He does this repetitive movement with joyous dexterity and intensity, setting up a rhythm impossible to describe in words and impossible for me, even with practice, to imitate well.

This stim is definitely socially inappropriate. In the beginning he was only forbidden to take a flapper outside the home. Now he is restricted to ten minutes of "flap time," once in the morning and once at night. However, workers on the morning shift have many times found Bruce's top drawer full of flapped pajama tops hastily stuffed back into place. Apparently James didn't want to mess up his own clothing.

Finally I went downstairs for a drink of ice water, while Otis took over sitting in their room. When I returned, he had James by the hand at the top of the stairs.

"What's he signing? Go ahead, James, tell her."

James signed "go" and "car."

"No, James, you're not going anywhere in a car. It's time for bed."

In response to that, James repeated his signs and gave Otis a little push and tried to lead him downstairs.

"Oh ho," I laughed. "Otis, he says it's time for *you* to go home in the car."

We put James back to bed.

"That's no dumb kid," I remarked.

"No," Otis agreed. "He's damn smart."

Saturday

It was only 6:15 A.M. when I turned off the house alarm, unlocked the front door, and went inside, but already I could hear the thunder of footsteps above my head. I grabbed some coffee and went up. It was Mack, resident early bird, waking the rest of the boys, including his roommate Sylvester.

Sylvester was going to be with us all weekend, his first in a while. He is twelve years old and supremely verbal; at the moment he was giving Mack a serious talking-to. I rescued Mack and told Sylvester to go watch television with the awake person. The rest of the boys went back to sleep.

At 8:00 I had to wake Bruce because he was going home in an hour. Although he had been wakened and taken to the toilet several times during the night, his pajamas and top sheet were soaked with urine. He was, as usual, hard to rouse. Once up, though, he was very calm and did not object to my quick washing of him with soap and a warm washcloth in the bathroom. Back in the bedroom, he perched, naked, on a pile of bedclothes on the floor and began lightly stroking his legs with his fingertips.

"Eat pan–cake?" he queried.

"We've got French toast today. But first you have to make your bed and get dressed."

"Eat pan–cake!" he emphasized and fell quiet again.

Meanwhile James had gotten up and I was trying to direct him through his bedmaking. Every few seconds he would stop to worry a loose tooth, or stare at the design on the radiator cover, or hold an index finger up to his right eye, seemingly trying to focus on it. I had to talk to him more and more, to his vocal annoyance, and eventually Bruce caught the tension in the room.

It was inevitable; Bruce seemed to catch tension the way a turtle catches flies. He sprang up, leaped across James's bed to the radiator, screaming in full voice, and then jumped over to the dresser top and started pulling down the curtains. I took him by the hands and got him quieted, trying to keep my voice low. Screaming at Bruce to stop screaming never works.

This sequence went on for almost ten minutes: quieting Bruce, directing James, chasing Bruce, quieting him—until James was finished with his work. James and I went down to start breakfast, and Dolores came in to be with Bruce. Once alone in the room, he would be better able to concentrate. Sometimes I think it is hard enough to be autistic without having an autistic roommate.

I worked with Sylvester all morning. His chores were sweeping and washing the back stairs and porch, loading the dishwasher, and folding his laundry. It was a tremendous strain on both of us—on him, because he had gotten out of the routine of weekend chores, on me, because he not only could argue better than the other boys (being so much more verbal), but he was also physically stronger. When he ran into the living room and collapsed into giggles on the couch, it was back-wrenching to pull him off. Then he pinched and poked you, not to hurt, just to annoy. And he found pieces of string, small balls of clay, anything, to chew or dangle from his lips.

At one point I shut the door between the back porch and the kitchen and threw my weight against it, Sylvester pounding and kicking the other side. But *finally* he got the porch and stairs passably clean, and then loaded the dishwasher with a serious look on his face, even disregarding Dolores's teasing. This chore he does extremely well, needing little or no prompting.

However, he balked at having to retrieve his laundry from the basement and fold it, and went all giggly on the couch again. I told him he would not eat lunch till it was done, nor would he be able to go on the community outing—roller skating. These threats motivated him to bring his laundry upstairs to the living room, but then he began picking up Rod's small toys. Rod loves to sit and stim with little blocks and such, by juggling them in his cupped palms until they spill out, or by tossing them higher and higher until they bounce off the ceiling. (At one time all the ceiling panels were dotted with holes made by his various projectiles.) Now, to Rod's vast amusement, Sylvester started throwing them behind the radiator. I grabbed Sylvester with his laundry and dragged him into a hidden corner of the room, out of sight of the rest of the house. He couldn't believe it. "Please!" he pleaded. "Let me out! I'll fold!"

"No way! Not until everybody's in the kitchen eating lunch!"

When he realized he couldn't push his way past me, he sat down and cried. Real tears. They didn't move me, either. When lunch began, I let him come out. He was subdued, but demanded I tell him which piece of clothing to fold first. I refused, saying he had to fold every piece, so the order didn't matter. He screamed, "Which one! Tell me which one!" I kept refusing to tell him.

After five minutes or so, the smell of chicken

noodle soup prompted him to fold all the clothing, in his own chosen order. We went in to lunch. I found myself relaxing after the stress of being with Sylvester all morning. Lincoln was doing a lot of his circular stimming with his head; he kept craning his head around, almost as if he were looking at something on the wall behind. I asked him to pass the salad; he responded by turning his head.

"It's on the table, Lincoln, not the wall!"

Lincoln, surprised, laughed. Dolores joined in now, too. She went over to peer at the wall.

"What's on here, anyway? What do you look for, bugs?"

I practiced his move. "No, he's pretending to be an owl."

Lincoln didn't say anything, but he was clearly amused. He's such a phony stimmer. He is twelve years old and not really autistic, at least not classically so. In fact, Otis refers to him as "one of your garden variety retarded." He does fit into the home, given his poor communication skills, which is fortunate for him. He has been institutionalized for so many years that the authorities were running out of places to put him. He talks frequently about the children on his ward in his previous placement, almost always asking with horror if they are going to show up. He was abused sexually there, mostly by boys.

His obsessions are Lawn-Boy lawnmowers and vacuum cleaners. We found out that for a long time he had carried around a picture of himself in diapers next to his father and their Lawn-Boy, so possibly he associates it with the only period of home life he knew. We also learned that as a child he had totally taken apart his mother's vacuum, an act for which he caught royal hell. He loves to fondle the hoses, and if given the chance, will hide them under his bed. He also loves to change the bags, both the grass-catcher on the lawnmower and the vacuum bags.

His parents are divorced and he visits each on alternate weekends. His father comes early for him, with another son in tow, and is pleased with Lincoln's progress. His mother comes late and brings him back early. She doesn't feel comfortable in his presence, and if Lincoln comes on a little threatening, she hurriedly drives him to the hardware store and lets him wander around in the mower section.

Sunday

Today Dolores was making pancakes with the little boys while I was going to chart Sylvester on changing his sheets. We were letting Rod lounge in bed till Susie came. However, he zipped into the bathroom, dunked his head into the toilet and started spouting water over the floor. He used the toilet water because the awake person routinely shuts off the sink water. Rod's absolutely favorite stim is water play, preferably in the bathroom. Many is the staff member who has gotten slugged or scratched while trying to disrupt Rod at the sink. He loves to get a mouthful and then, on his toes, hands twisting and turning between his legs in glee, spout it up and into the wastebasket or the toilet.

I hollered at him and he whined, closing the

door. Everytime I pushed it open, he came at me menacingly and slammed it shut. After a few repetitions I was scared his behavior would escalate into a full tantrum, so dangerous in the bathroom. I went downstairs, feeling slightly humiliated, to ask Dolores to change places.

I am totally ineffective with Rod, mostly because he scares the daylights out of me. It isn't the fear of being hurt, because the other boys hurt me. I think the difference is that I have relationships with them, however "autistic," and the pain becomes more understandable, but I've never felt comfortable with Rod. He gets a menacing look in his eyes, and I'm terrified.

Lincoln used to scare me, too, when he first moved in and was testing us a lot with belligerent, running-away behaviors. I worked my way out of that fear by talking to him every chance I got, by getting to know him, by developing a rapport. Rod's rages are more organic, and I have yet to face my fear of him.

We were preparing to go for a picnic lunch in the park. The lunches were made; everything looked ready. Sylvester had yet to put on his shoes and jacket, and he was acting preposterously silly in the living room, poking his fingers at the staff, giggling, and jumping on the couch. I warned him:

"Sylvester, I'll stay here with you if you don't get your act together. You'll have to miss the picnic."

He didn't believe me. Yesterday we had threatened up to the last possible second that he would miss roller skating, but had lacked enough staff to carry the threat out. We let him return to our good graces by behaving and apologizing in that last possible second.

Today I fully intended to stay home if necessary, and repeatedly told Sylvester that. The other kids and staff began to file out the front door.

"Hey, stop, wait for me! I'll put on my shoes! I'll behave! Please!"

"No, Sylvester. Bye! We're going to have a good time at the park, and you missed out!"

"No, wait, I'll be good; I'm sorry."

"Bye!"

He couldn't believe his eyes. Everyone left the house but us. He hopped up and down in front of the locked door, trying to change my mind. I had to drag him away from it.

We spent the time, except for a quick sandwich, in the basement doing laundry. This chore, done by each boy every weekend, was nobody's favorite. Sylvester kept running into the furnace room, slamming the door behind him, and banging on the pipes. It was nerve-wracking. At one point I wondered what in *hell* I was doing on a beautiful summer Sunday, alone in the basement of a huge house except for a twelve-year-old boy, whom I had to drag from the furnace to the dryer, from the furnace to the dryer, over and over again.

I kept my patience, however, until we had gone upstairs and Sylvester was messing up the staff office, which is off limits to the kids. He slammed my pinky finger in the top drawer of the desk; I really got angry and screamed at him.

The afternoon staff was planning to go to the

zoo. On pain of losing this outing, too, Sylvester folded his laundry *and* Lincoln's, and went upstairs, independently, to put everything away.

Staff Meeting

The new executive director says the house was a mess one morning when visitors from another agency came. The upstairs was so bad that it embarrassed him. He had composed a list of infractions, one of which was socks, balled up, on the awake-room floor.

"Oh," several staff members immediately rejoined, "Those aren't *socks*, those are James's flappers!"

There are socks—and then there are flappers: several balled-up ones inserted into a stretched-out tube sock, which is then knotted at the end, and all twisted from flapping. How could anyone mistake one for the other?

Well, uh, whatever, mumbled our new leader.

Saturday

All the boys were going home or out with family, except for Rod, so the first few hours were a flurry of activity getting everyone ready.

Bruce was extremely tense and screamy. Told to set the table, he got on top and walked on it, instead. When finally breakfast was ready, he put maybe six bites of French toast in his mouth, chewed, and then spat it all out again, asking "More honey?"

"No way. You're just sucking it off."

Later in the living room, I made him sit by me while I read several storybooks. Bruce enjoys looking at books and being read to; he knows all the

Sesame Street and Charlie Brown characters. He certainly does not read spontaneously; however, they may force him to do so at school. He just likes to carry around a book and gnaw at its corners. Staff memos on him usually carry the (almost) tongue-in-cheek instruction: "If you see Bruce eating a book, take it away from him." After a few minutes, although his body still felt electric, he came back into focus and stopped screaming and climbing the furniture.

By the time Bruce's mother came to fetch him, however, I was not in the house but in the backyard with Sylvester, having exchanged places with Dolores at her request. The unofficial rule is to ask to switch off with a staff member after twenty minutes or so, if you are having a hard time. Sometimes I have trouble complying with this rule, since it seems like admitting defeat; that, of course, is just an ego problem. Often the child and the adult are so locked into each other that the only way to break the deadlock is for a new adult to step in, and then often the breakthrough is immediate.

Anyway, Sylvester had been scheduled to go home the night before, but because he had refused to do his work and had gone on a two-hour silliness binge, Dolores had called his parents to delay their coming. Dolores took these things seriously. At the moment he was supposed to be putting the garbage out behind the garage. He was balking, trying to get back into the house and meeting Dolores's resistance. In his frustration, he knocked over the picnic table and broke off its legs.

As I took over, Dolores told me not to interact

with him verbally, because he knew what he had to do, and he would just be trying to manipulate me. So I didn't say a word. I did protect myself from his pinches, dodge the rocks he threw at my head, and pull him down from the fence. At one point I read a newspaper front to back while he jabbered with a toddler who was watching us from his apartment window next door. Sylvester complained to him about me, and all the work he had to do, and the toddler grinned at Sylvester, and held up various toys, strings, and pieces of dirt for his inspection.

Later, when I was chasing Sylvester from one end of the yard to the other, trying to prevent his escape out the gates, I would look up at the window as I passed. Each time the baby would point in the appropriate direction and solemnly tell me, "Go!" He was vastly interested in our goings-on.

When his mother did show up, Sylvester had a distinct change of attitude and worked like a beaver.

Rod has a new weekend behavior therapist, Vanette. (Susie works Monday through Friday). I went with them for a picnic lunch at the park. Rod did his usual tricks of twisting two swings together to watch them unswing, and spitting water from the water fountain, so Vanette marched him, whining, home. He tossed a rock along the way, and when he went to pick it up again, Vanette stepped on it. He tried to vent his frustration by swiping at me, but she intervened and pushed his arm away. She'll be all right! Better than me, already.

Later, the kids straggled home again and we turned on the hose in the backyard. Mack was frightened at first, I think because he didn't want his face to get wet, but then he backed into the spray, slowly, with a big smile on his face.

Sunday

Dolores asked me to do Bruce's laundry with him. Bruce was in the kitchen. After I told him what we were going to do, he smacked me, hard, on the breast, screamed, and pulled my hair. I caught him by the wrists and sat him down on a chair. After several calm seconds, I let his hands go. He immediately jumped up onto the table and scampered around it, just out of my reach. When I did get him down, he grabbed the tablecloth and pulled it onto the floor. I told him to replace it; he jumped up on the table again.

Possibly at this point I should have removed him from the room and sat him down till he was calm, for *sure*, but I decided not to. He was *so* wound up I decided to work through it. I had him get a sponge to clean the table before replacing the cloth. He attempted to eat the sponge. I took it out of his mouth.

Finally he calmed sufficiently to clean the table, replace the cloth, and fetch his laundry basket from his closet. In the basement, however, he became extremely rigid and tense again. He stood and stared at the clothes while I asked him, repeatedly, to load the washer. I kept breaking down the steps for him until at last I said, "Bruce, bend over," and he leaned over the basket, at which point he seemed able to continue the sequence by himself. After each article of clothing dropped into the washer, he slammed down the lid as if in anger. When it was time to measure the soap, he would feign scooping the cup in the box but then would come up with nothing. He held it to his lips as if to sip, and then began putting the soap in his mouth. Quickly I held his hand on the cup to measure a cupful and dump it in the machine. He ran his fingers along the inside of the agitator and sucked the soap off.

I took him upstairs and told him to brush his teeth. He threw his toothbrush behind the radiator. I washed his mouth out with my own hands. When he got away from me, he jumped into the bathtub.

Our afternoon outing began with a picnic. Dolores said to have James make peanut-butter crackers instead of sandwiches, because he didn't eat sandwiches.

"Oh yes, he does," I told her, "although he'll complain. Otis said we shouldn't cater to that."

"O–kay!"

The big moment came. James took the sandwich out of the bag. He started to peel the bread apart.

"Ah–ah–ah! Eat it like a sandwich!"

He took a bite, properly, and chewed it as if he were gagging on poison.

"Very good, James! I like the way you're eating that sandwich!"

And so on, tiny piece by tiny piece, pained look by pained look, until it was all eaten. A small success, I guess. But still a success. And Otis, for all his tough-guy attitude which pained our soft hearts, had been right. Sometimes you cannot tell what these boys are capable of, until you sit on them a little.

Saturday

Sylvester was watching television with the awake person when I arrived and was not enthusiastic about the prospect of changing his sheets. Watching television had been Sylvester's major stim before he came to the group home. He had program schedules, plots, characters, all memorized, and talked about them incessantly. We had immediately reduced his "tube time," but on Saturday mornings it is always difficult to dislodge him.

Mack was dressing and making his bed, and I was charting him, so my attention was divided. I kept turning off the set, but whenever I went back to Mack, Sylvester would turn it on. When I resorted to unplugging it, he plugged it back in. Finally Mack was finished and I could devote my energy to Sylvester. To his utter horror I picked up the television and put it in James and Bruce's room.

Sylvester knew I meant business, but I surely ruined Bruce's morning. Here he was just waking up, and there was a television set hidden behind the lounge chair and Sylvester crying at the doorway. Bruce jumped out of bed and leaped over to the chair, screaming "Watch tee vee!"

When Sylvester gave up trying to barge past me to get to the tube, he stood crying for a moment and then turned and dashed downstairs. By the time I got there, he was comfortably ensconced on the couch next to Vanette, watching cartoons on the downstairs set.

"Oh no, you don't!" And I grabbed him and dragged him halfway back upstairs, pausing on the way to let Rod's mother in the front door.

"Good morning," I mustered cheerily.

"Good morning," she returned, giving me a sympathetic expression.

"Hi!" screeched Sylvester, pinching my wrists continuously.

"Good morning, Sylvester."

Dolores found us on the stairs a minute later and she took over for me. When I returned, a half hour later, they were still tussling on the exact same stair.

"Help me get him into his room, will you?"

Sylvester howled and yowled, mostly in amusement, while we carried him into his room.

"I'll take over for awhile," I said, as Sylvester slammed the door in Dolores's face. The doorknob fell off.

"Well, now we're stuck in here. When your bed's done, I'll call for somebody to come get us."

"O–pen the *door!*"

"I can't! It's broken! You'll just have to work."

I couldn't help laughing. Both the doorknob's falling off and Sylvester's disbelief struck me as extremely funny.

"Do–*lor*–es! Do–*lor*–es! Help!"

Naturally Dolores ignored his cries, never dreaming we actually *might* need her help. Sylvester often cried wolf. His best trick was to lean out of his window, screaming "Stop it! Stop it! Stop *hitting* me!" to anyone who cared to listen, while the staff member was on the other side of the room, wanting but not daring to tear Sylvester limb from limb.

I sat down on Mack's bed to rest. Sylvester started kicking the door. Smash! Smash! He was angry; I ignored him. After five minutes or so he discovered a small strip of peeling paint on the door and finished peeling it off. Then he started pulling at other spots, rolling the paint into little balls which he put in his mouth and chewed as if they were gum.

"Sylvester, you will have to pay for someone to repaint your door. Do you have any money?"

"No."

"Well, then you'll have to work to earn it."

"But I want to get *out* of here!"

"Then change your bed."

His reply was to deliver a series of savage kicks to the door.

"And if you break the door, you'll have to pay to fix it."

And on and on we went. Finally he lay down on his bed and delivered a self-pitying soliloquy. He informed me that he felt like a dead crow, which proved wrong my hypothesis that although Sylvester talked a lot, he talked only concretely and was incapable of abstraction.

I sat against the door, my head on my knees. I grew sleepier and sleepier—Sylvester could be so damn boring—until, I confess, I dozed off, waking up with a jerk as Sylvester tried to get past me. It was awful to have fallen asleep like that, but at least I felt refreshed. We tussled a bit longer and then Sylvester decided to work.

Dolores opened the door for us afterward, at my request, and we went downstairs for lunch. I heard Sylvester complain to James:

"They treat me like a telephone. Am I a man or a telephone? James! Am I a man or a telephone?"

James just kept on flapping his sock.

Sylvester looked over at me. I silently held my fingers up to my ear in the sign for "telephone." Leaning against the wall, arms folded akimbo across his chest, Sylvester gave me a *very* scornful look and dropped the subject.

Sunday

The community pool was open for the summer. After lunch Vanette and I headed over with Rod, James, and Mack. I hadn't brought a suit, but Vanette had hers, and the attendant said it was okay for me to walk around in bare feet and shorts, but not to go in the water. I was leery at this inadequate coverage of our kids, but two staff members were coming to replace me in an hour when my shift was over.

James jumped right in. He was a genuine fish. Mack stood in the shallowest part and grabbed onto the side, happy but cautious. Rod jumped right in, too, and started gulping and spouting as he paddled across to the other side. Vanette followed him.

Mack looked pretty self-sufficient, since the water was only halfway up his shins. I had to follow James.

There was a slide which he entered from the water end, illegally. Then he tried to go down it on his belly, also illegally. Children and lifeguards were screaming at him and at each other to nab the miscreant. Luckily I got to him first. I turned him onto his butt, and he slid down giggling.

"He's handicapped," I explained tersely to the girl with the whistle around her neck. "He doesn't talk, but he understands everything you say to him."

She nodded sympathetically. "I'll keep an eye on him for you."

She did, too, I guess, but it didn't matter for very long, because soon James paddled across to the deeper side of the pool, where Rod was still spouting and being avoided by wondering children. I went around to stand with Vanette, my eyes still back on Mack, by now out of my voice range. He had staked out his territory, as usual, and was traversing it—about fifteen feet from either side of the spot where he had entered the pool.

The only problem was that several mothers were sitting on the edge, watching their kids. Mack ignored them completely, but got right smack up against their knees as he reached around them to grab onto the rim of the pool. They were giving him strange looks and tucking their suit skirts around their thighs.

My bigger worry was that if I took my eyes off him he would sink down and drown before I looked again. Consequently I wasn't paying sufficient attention to James, who was directly underneath me, trying to flap the metal pool ladder. Vanette was telling him to stop, but I figured it was a harmless activity so long as nobody wanted to use it "appropriately," so I was keeping out of their argument. All of a sudden, I looked down for him, and he wasn't there.

"James! Where'd he go?" I shouted to Vanette as I paced around, staring into the water, expecting to see his lifeless body floating slowly to the surface.

"I don't see him!" I was on the edge of panic.

"There he is!" Vanette pointed.

Although swimming the length of the diving pool was forbidden, James had done exactly that and was now on the top rung of the ladder of the highest diving board. Another child was still on the end preparing to jump, another rule James had broken. The children around the diving pool were all pointing and screaming; three or four lifeguards were blowing their whistles. As I strode around the pool to fetch him, everyone grew quiet and the child went ahead and took his dive. When I got close enough, I yelled, "James! Come down from there!" And he grinned at me just before his feet left the end of the board.

"He can't do that," the handsome lifeguard told me impassively as we watched James chugging around the middle of the diving pool.

"I know. He's handicapped. Once I can get him, he'll stay out, I promise."

I could see James was tiring because he kept heading for the edge. After all, the water was ten feet deep. Everytime he got close enough for me to snatch him, though, he grinned at me and then treaded out toward the middle again. He had obviously figured out that since I wasn't wearing a suit,

I wouldn't be going in to fetch him. I didn't want anybody else to try, even though I had some volunteers, because I didn't want them getting scratched or bitten. I just stood there, waiting, with everyone watching my complete lack of control over this kid, until finally his fatigue got the better of him. He swam to a ladder and came out independently.

"Boy," the handsome lifeguard said to me, "He might be handicapped, but he sure as hell can swim!"

Friday

I worked the awake shift tonight, beginning it early—at 8:00 instead of 10:00—so the kids were still taking showers and doing laundry. Lucy told me Bruce's EEG results came back: grand mal seizures.

I couldn't believe it. I couldn't associate the most bizarre of Bruce's behavior with my admittedly scanty experience of grand mal seizures. Petit mal would have surprised me less, because Bruce did have momentary periods of blankness and rigidity. I was supposed to give him his shower, but I couldn't. He was acting really spacy, and I was totally ineffective. I kept thinking, is he seizing now? Now? And of what use is verbal correction during a seizure? Dolores finally came to my rescue and worked him through his shower. Verbally.

James was asleep when Bruce went to bed, tucked in by another staff member. I went in the room to relieve her, and Bruce reached up for me. I thought he wanted a hug, but he pulled me down on the bed.

"Sleep?" he chirped.

"Now that is very rare—for Bruce to want anyone to lie down with him. Usually he pushes me away when I sit down next to him."

"Is it against the rules?" I asked, starting to get up.

"No, no, it's fine. Stay there. I'm going home."

"Goodnight."

I lay there with Bruce, touched by his unusual display of affection. He even held my hand and stroked my fingers. My feeling soon changed to one of annoyance, however, for as he started to relax to sleep, he continuously snuffed his nose and smacked his lips directly in my ear. I was tired and the noise really annoyed me. I prayed he would fall asleep quickly, because I wanted to stay as he had asked me to do. After about ten minutes, he did sleep and I moved out into the awake room.

Immediately Lincoln came out of his room. Obviously he had been waiting for me. The week before, he had cut the bottom of his foot, requiring a trip to the hospital for stitches. It must have been all the glory of the attention that made Lincoln refuse to let his cut heal. He kept ripping his bandage off and dragging his foot along the floor. Now his bandage was off and his cut had reopened again.

Dolores appeared, too, with plates of omelets and mugs of coffee. The eggs cooled while she rebandaged his foot. Then she made him sit up straight in the chair and watch us while we ate.

"And take that thumb out of your mouth, Lincoln!"

Saturday

My day's work seemed consumed by James's bowel movements. Or lack thereof.

James had his own way of elimination. He lifted up the toilet seat and dipped his butt right in the water. Then he would put his hands in and flap the water about; afterward he might flap and/or eat his feces. After cleaning up several of *these* horrendous messes, the staff had stopped his flapping by demanding his hands be kept on his knees during the whole process.

Now we were trying to stop his butt-dipping (BD, for short). James was crafty, however. Whenever left unguarded for the shortest second, he would run to the bathroom on another floor of the house, including the houseparent's in the basement if left unlocked, and BD till he had relieved himself or someone caught him.

This morning he really was full up, and had to go badly, but he held it in steadfastly rather than keep his rear out of the water. I lost track of the times I ran up and down the stairs chasing him out of bathrooms, and the times I made him wash his fingers and face because he had inserted his finger in himself.

"James, wash the *crap* off your nose!"

At lunch he drank a big glass of grape juice, so I figured I had him. I made him sit correctly on the toilet. "Now you stay here, James, till you poop." It was so close to coming out I had gravity on my side if nothing else.

For half an hour he sat and laughed at some internal joke and shook his hands by his eyes and flicked his feet together. Several times he bounced up exuberantly and began a jumping dance, but I redirected him back to the seat.

"You may *not* get off the toilet until I see some crap in that bowl!"

I was, I suppose, unprofessionally graphic.

"Push!"

He pushed, he really did, and every single drop of urine he had must have dripped out, but no poop. It was as if he couldn't relax his anus without water splashing it.

Finally I had to answer the phone and he popped off, carefully flushing two or three times behind himself. I let him go.

An outsider would probably not believe the intensity of the discussion generated among the staff by James's unorthodox bowel habits. We once had quite an argument over the pros and cons of BDing; the con side included the dangers of ever taking James to a forest preserve. If he were to attempt a BD in an outhouse . . . well, the mind boggles.

Sunday

All the kids were home, unusual for a Sunday morning, yet the day was unusually uneventful. We took them to a softball game nearby, and tried to teach them to clap and cheer at appropriate times, to my mind an absurd undertaking. Lincoln decided to run away, but Dolores had crept down the bleachers behind him. Consequently, they had an intense sprint around the whole bleacher section, and Lincoln came back to sit beside me as if nothing had happened. Dolores was panting.

"You looked ridiculous," I teased her. An occupational hazard.

The sun was very hot. James kept signing to me

for something to drink, but there was nothing for sale except for orange sugar-water which I refused to let him have. (The boys get *really* hyperactive on sugar.) Mack and Rod were staying at the park after the game, with Vanette, to have a picnic. James knew there was food in their big paper sack. He kept heading in its direction. Finally the game was over and we started home. James couldn't understand why *he* couldn't partake of the picnic. I explained to him that we would eat lunch as soon as we got home, but he was just too hot and frustrated. He grabbed my forearm and sunk his teeth in. The ensuing walk home was not too pleasant.

I had James make himself a peanut-butter sandwich for lunch. With only a little prompting he ate the whole damn thing correctly.

Friday

I went to work for a few hours tonight, from 5:00 to 10:00 P.M., not the most energetic time of my day. I was hot, tired, and hungry when I arrived on my bicycle, my eyes smarting from all the rush-hour car fumes. Wearily I climbed the stairs to the front porch. I met the houseparents there, incoming and outgoing. Dolores is quitting, to pursue other, more peaceful interests. I am very sorry to see her go. Her last day is tomorrow; a newcomer, Sanford, is taking her place.

To my surprise Sylvester was sitting on the other end of the porch floor, quietly, arms on his crossed legs. He grinned at me, wordlessly, but so in tune with my spirit that I grinned back, all my fatigue banished by that silent exchange which seemed to convey so much understanding. How my life would be diminished if I didn't have these kids in it!

Sylvester and I went food shopping, while everyone else prepared dinner. It was a first time for me, so I told Sylvester to lead the way. He did, impressing me with his independence as he read his list and picked out the items. His only trouble came when the quantity wasn't indicated; then he picked out one. One loaf of bread, one can of juice.

He was really less conspicuous than I was, standing in front of the meat counter with a clipboard and pen in hand. However, he did stand too close to other people, practically breathing down a woman's neck as he inspected the contents of her cart. He talked to himself the whole time, which might have been all right, except that he often addressed the ceiling, gesturing expansively.

Dinner was vegetarian: a vegetable-cheese casserole. Dessert was chocolate cake, homemade by a staff member in honor of Dolores's last night. Now Mack is a superb eater, except that he is allergic to tomatoes and he detests zucchini. You could set him off into a lengthy tirade just by mentioning the word: "*No eat zucchini!*" After he dished himself out a big spoonful of the casserole and caught sight of the zucchini slices floating in the sauce, he began his squawking. I was about to move the offensive pieces to the side of the plate when Dolores stopped me.

"Mack, if you want chocolate cake, you will eat every bite of zucchini."

"No eat zucchini."

"Oh Mack, it's not really zucchini, it's Italian squash," I fibbed.

"No squash, no zucchini."

"Mack, Italian squash is good! And then you'll get chocolate cake."

Anything chocolate is a great motivator for Mack. His mother used to make him work all week for chocolate doughnuts on Saturday morning, and although *we* don't stoop to food bribery, still. . . . He cocked his head sideways at me, squinted, and put a piece of Italian squash in his mouth. He grimaced, gagged, and finally swallowed.

"All right, Mack!"

I had to turn my attention to James, who was sitting on my other side. When I turned back to Mack, every zucchini slice was gone! I couldn't believe it.

"Give this kid a giant piece of chocolate cake!"

After dinner we tried to motivate James similarly. He wanted a second helping of cake. We said no, and he went into the bathroom. I told him he *could* have a second helping, if he had a proper bowel movement. He tried, but no luck. Finally I told him to pull his pants up, and stuck my head out the bathroom door to say something to Dolores. By the time I pulled my head back in, he had butt-dipped an enormous movement.

"Into the shower, James. You cleaned yourself out, but you didn't earn the cake."

Bruce has now been on medication to control his seizures for a few days. His body has lost a lot of its rigidity, and he seemed to be able to relax to sleep more quickly. However, one evening's observation counts for very little, especially with these kids.

Saturday

A horrendous day. Sanford took over from Dolores at 9:00 A.M. and parents were in and out all morning. At one point I was trying to read to Bruce on the couch to keep him from screaming and climbing because he thought (as we all did) that his mother was coming (a misunderstanding; she wasn't), and keep James from running to snitch food or butt-dip or flap the drawstring out of his swimming suit while waiting for his mom to finish talking with the director. Meanwhile Rod's mother was sitting and watching me intently, and Rod kept taking Bruce's book out of my hands so I would thank him for giving it back. Mayhem!

Sanford was having his troubles with Sylvester and Lincoln, who had banded together to test the new man in the house. At one point he left them both upstairs till they were ready to come down and work. I knew it was a mistake to leave even two of the "big boys" alone and unattended, but hesitated to intervene. After I could stand the suspense no longer, I went upstairs. Lincoln was masturbating; Sylvester was watching television.

"Okay you guys, fun time is over!"

By lunch Sanford was dead tired. Although he had worked in a classroom with autistic children, his group-home experience had been with mentally retarded adults, so this environment was a different story for him.

"You really almost need one-on-one with these kids, don't you?" he muttered to me in a surprised tone. I just laughed.

Sunday

This morning, as often happens, all the children except James were being kept fairly well occupied. He was either flapping or getting into trouble, and I was tired of the same old interactions with him. I decided to devote my day's attention to his work. I had him vacuum the living room, dust all the furniture, wash windows, and scrub two bathroom floors. He worked very well, except for several chases down into the houseparent's bathroom.

The second time I didn't run fast enough and he successfully butt-dipped. What bothered me more than the BD was his insistence on sticking his dirty finger up his nose immediately afterward. He wouldn't even take it out long enough to pull up his pants, let alone wash. Every time I took his hand down, he put it right back in. Finally he attempted to bite my arm. I sat him down on the floor to gain better control, and he attempted to bite his own upper arm—a common enough action for several of the other boys, but not for James. Then he did something I have never observed him do—throw his head down backward onto the floor, not once but twice, before I stopped him by letting go of his hands and holding his head tightly.

"James, I know you're angry, but I will *not* let you hurt yourself. Now sit up." He sat up. After I saw he was quieted, I told him to fix his pants and wash. He did both and then trotted back upstairs.

For lunch he ate three hot dogs, with me guiding every bite to make sure he always got bun and meat together.

Right before I was ready to leave, he came hurtling inside from the backyard, signing his own weak "water" sign. He went into the bathroom and got a plastic cup, verbalizing a little song, in which I thought I detected a sound not unlike "wa–ter."

"Say water, James. Water! You want WATER! WATER! WATER! WATER!" I shouted it right in his ear. "Go on! WA–TER! WA–TER! WA–TER!"

He loved it. He even stopped drinking and turned to laugh at me, making a tentative sound with his lips. It was the wrong sound, but he was trying. That's all you can ask.

Friday

Today the kids were off from summer school because of a holiday, so I worked six hours, from 9:00 A.M. till 3:00 P.M. When I arrived, they had already dressed and eaten; I got a break from kitchen chores. In fact, Sanford asked me to take James and Bruce to the park, giving me an easy morning.

As always, I held Bruce's hand, because he has a penchant for making terrifically fast dashes into the street. James does fairly well under verbal control on walks, except for peeling up wads of bubble gum off the sidewalk and eating them. No matter how loudly you scream, he keeps on peeling and eating.

At the park, all our kids alternate between appropriate and idiosyncratic play, with Bruce playing the least. He occasionally swings or climbs a little, but mostly sits with staff, asking "go home?" or "take a walk?" or runs out of the play area into the parking lot. Today he sat down quietly next to me on the bench and held my arm around him. James rode a horse-swing and climbed a bit, stuck his nose in the garbage can to get a good whiff, and then plunked himself on my lap, lifting his shirt for a scratch. We looked a contented trio.

We sat there quietly in the sunshine for an unusually long time, given these kids' supposed inability to form relationships with others. I felt that perhaps because of all the new staff at the home, James and Bruce were appreciating some peaceful moments with an old-timer, a known quantity in their lives. I also realized how much I value my relationships with the six boys, and how intimately I have gotten to know them in eleven months, an intimacy impossible to rush.

Our interlude did not, of course, last forever. James sank down on his knees, scooping up dirt and heaving it back through his legs exactly like a puppy dog, incidentally showering me. Bruce asked for "drink of water"; I took him to the fountain. He turned it on full force and got slurped in the face. He screamed. I helped him, but it took a few minutes to get his courage up to try again. Meanwhile James was trying to tip the huge garbage can over; I prayed Bruce would finish his drink before James succeeded. Luckily he did. I got James redirected toward the swings. When I turned around, Bruce was running toward the parking lot. I ran to retrieve him. Meanwhile James found a ground-in wad of gum. Etc. Etc. Etc.

Saturday

I arrived at 6:30 A.M. and already the noise was terrific. Quickly I headed upstairs. Lincoln and Rod were asleep, but Sylvester and Mack were wrestling in their room and I could hear James and Bruce screaming, screaming in theirs. Sanford emerged, shaking his head.

As I went in, the awake person was holding a pair of pajama bottoms out to a naked Bruce, who was sitting on his bed, screeching. Bruce wouldn't even look at the pajamas, and the awake person was obviously out of patience. He jerked Bruce's arm and said, "C'mon, Bruce, put them on."

I was out of patience with the awake person who, in all fairness, did not have enough genuine awake time with the boys to build up a working relationship. Plus, the graveyard shift was not easy to fill, let alone with truly qualified and sensitive people.

"You don't have to jerk his arm out of joint. He doesn't need to put those on anyway."

"Well, he wet. He's been wetting all night."

"Okay, Bruce, let's go get washed off."

Bruce came into the bathroom with me. No washcloths. I knew he wouldn't wait for me to get one downstairs, so I washed him with a pillowcase. He didn't like it.

James had been up practically all night, the awake person informed me: flapping and urinating. I looked at James. He was kicking the radiator to hear the wonderful noise it made. His eyes did look pretty bleary.

Finally Sanford and the awake person went to separate Sylvester and Mack, allowing me to calm Bruce and James down. I let James lie in bed, but quietly, so I could concentrate on getting Bruce ready for a home visit. He didn't dress immediately, but he did stop the screaming. Both boys, like yesterday in the park, seemed to respond to a calm, firm presence from whom they know what to expect. It was good for me to have these few moments of feeling adequate and competent; they certainly didn't happen too often.

After breakfast came chore time. Sanford was having a hard time getting Lincoln and Sylvester to work. His problem is that he speaks with them as if they were mentally retarded adults, who are as a rule more cooperative, polite, and talkative than autistic children. He is so surprised here when he asks, "Sylvester, do you want to load the dishwasher?" and the reply is invariably, "No!" Or he comes into the living room and asks "Who wants to help me clean the kitchen?" Silence.

Today Sylvester gets totally out of control by being silly and running away from his work. Sanford begins politely enough but grows increasingly firm. The insight is dawning that giving Sylvester all the free time he wants *before* his chores only postpones the clash. He offers him, instead, a bike ride *after* the work. The staff is, in fact, just about to begin a program with Sylvester. On the weekends he must write down his list of chores and his own chosen reward, like a bicycle ride with a staff member or coloring time.

Sylvester loves to color. His pictures are very perseverative, always the same: rows of numbers either circled or put into a long frame, like a baseball score. He colors in each number and sometimes adds a word to two, like "cool" or "high." He talks to each crayon as he chooses it, often as part of a running game-show patter. I have sat for an entire hour with him while he colored picture after picture and kept up a literally nonstop verbal barrage. He talked not to me, but to the crayons and numbers. He did, however, ask me to participate in applauding a number who has won a prize, or has stood up as "the real number three."

Today, however, there is no coloring time. For almost four hours, Sanford and I take turns sitting with Sylvester either on the couch or on the back porch waiting for him to quiet down enough to sweep and mop the porch. Finally it is the threat of missing fireworks tonight that makes him begin.

Sunday

Because of the Fourth of July fireworks last night, the kids went to bed very late and were still sleeping when I arrived. It was almost eight o'clock when Mack and Sylvester awoke. Sanford told them they could watch television upstairs till 8:30. They plopped themselves on the couch: Sylvester attentive to Mr. Rogers, Mack attentive to his own genitals sticking out of his pajama bottoms, thinking his own thoughts.

I called to Mack to come sit with me on the lounge chair. He came immediately and cuddled himself in my arms, still ignoring the tube. I have never seen him concentrate on the screen, unless someone calls his attention to it.

Sylvester watches cartoons with a complete lack of expression on his face and his eyelids half-closed. Frequently I tell him his brain is going to turn to oatmeal from watching so much television, a threat he repeats with amusement. Today, however, he was really responding to Mr. Rogers, talking back to the set to answer his greeting and various questions he posed. This is the kind of show Sylvester needs; it is the only one which makes him more alert and focused, rather than less so.

Afterward I went in their room with them for dressing and bedmaking. Sylvester was recalcitrant, but not exceedingly so. He said, anyway, that it was the polar bear who was misbehaving. Just before going down to breakfast, he asked me if I believed him about the polar bear. Before I could answer, he announced:

"There is no polar bear! He's in my head. My imagination!" I was impressed.

When we got downstairs, Vanette and Rod had already started lunch. She had come armed with cookbooks this morning and was planning chili and dutch apple pie for lunch, a banana cream pie for dinner's dessert. Immediately she told me to get James out of the kitchen.

"I can't stand that kid in here! He's a spoiled brat. He's the one who needs the one-on-one behavior therapist."

"That's because he's a food snitcher, and food happens to be your thing!"

"Well . . ."

"Well. . . . Food snitching's rather harmless compared to Bruce's furniture-climbing and screaming. You can make a case for any of these kids."

"All the same, get him out of here."

Each of us brings our own particular neurosis to the group home; Vanette's happens to be one of the more overt ones. The bad part is that she is wasting Rod's time this morning, since, of course, she won't let him do anything except watch and clean up.

Later, on the way to the park, Sylvester again explained to me about all the people and animals in his head.

"Who's been teaching you about imagination?"

"Mister Rogers."

At the park I heard him earnestly talking to Sanford about the number five, a frequent preoccupation of his. He counts to four and tries to prevent five from popping out. Sometimes it pops, sometimes not. Sanford was thoroughly confused. Then Sylvester came over to continue the talk with me.

"I don't know if five will pop out this time or not!"

"Well, you never know. Let's try it."

We alternated numbers. Five remained unpopped. We did it several times to make sure.

Sanford looked at me in disbelief that I would join in such inappropriate play, but I was trying to show him how to relax with Sylvester on *his* level, so we weren't always the big, mean authority figures. Besides, when he's not being a pill, Sylvester can be a lot of fun. I have sometimes imagined when he and I are alone at the park, swinging and singing songs, that we are brother and sister.

For a few minutes before lunch, I supervised James coloring upstairs. I love to watch him color; the results are pure energy. I offered him some colored chalk. At first he didn't like it because it kept breaking, or ripping the thin paper, but then he discovered some cardboard, which didn't give way under the pressure. He really responded to the texture he built up by layering his chalk strokes. When a piece broke, he pushed it onto the floor and picked up a new one. When he was finished, a new box of chalks had been reduced to a pile of tiny fragments.

Lunch went well. James ate two huge bowls of chili, four baking-powder biscuits, and a giant slice of apple pie. I was glad I wouldn't be on toilet watch with him later in the day.

Just before leaving I smelled bananas on his breath. I peeked in the refrigerator. The banana cream pie, in a large rectangular pan, had a familiar hand swipe across it. I didn't have the heart to tell Vanette.

It was exactly at my point of departure that a catastrophe almost happened. Everyone was on the front porch waiting to go swimming. Rod's parents and little brother were there, too. I was at the side of the house unlocking my bike when I saw James run into a street full of cars, so full, fortunately, that they weren't going too fast. I screamed at him, but he was beyond reach. Sanford ran after him and reached him just as a car slammed on its brakes, missing him by inches.

Everyone on the porch was either shrieking or stunned into silence. After talking with the driver (poor woman!), Sanford, looking shaken, brought James back. I immediately charged over and grabbed James, practically throwing him to the ground. I sat on him so I would have his complete attention while I hollered.

"You will never *never* NEVER run into that street again! You could have been hurt!" Etc. Etc. James nodded his head a mile a minute.

"All right, you go sit on the steps with your hands on your knees. You do not *move* until time for swimming!"

At least, as was commented later, he might want to avoid being screamed at by a raving technician the next time he thinks of running streetward. I hope so.

Saturday

Today the air-conditioning unit was being installed and necessary rewiring done, so we had to be out of the house from 9:00 A.M. till 4:00 P.M. We planned a breakfast at McDonalds and then a zoo excursion, which entailed a long train and bus ride both ways. This schedule was enough to motivate the little guys—Mack, Bruce, and James; Vanette woke up Rod who was cranky about the whole thing. Sylvester was home for the weekend; Sanford was tackling Lincoln, a late sleeper.

Lincoln was supposed to be home with his mother all weekend. However, after two hours on Friday night, she called Sanford and said she was bringing him back. Lincoln's new craze is boxing and apparently he punched her around a bit. He explained to her that he was being playful, but she didn't appreciate it. So now all Lincoln has to do to come back to the group home early from a weekend with Mom is to punch her. Or probably even threaten to punch her. Nobody thought to give him a different consequence.

Anyway, this morning Lincoln kept whining and saying he wanted to stay in bed all day, but miraculously we were out of the house only a few minutes behind schedule. James did take the time to stick his hand in the box of pastries his father had brought for the workers' breakfast, and Bruce managed to splash his anti-seizure medication all over his clothes and the kitchen sink.

Rod and Vanette had their own table at McDonalds. The rest of us squeezed into a booth. Sanford took the orders: pancakes for everyone but Mack, who announced he wanted "scrambled eggs." (He acts so damn mature, sometimes.) I secretly ordered a doughnut, which Lincoln discovered and bounced across my tray to watch the powdered sugar fly off.

Everyone needed help cutting the huge pancakes; I felt as if my elbows were poking out all over the table. There were no less than three syrup pitchers; naturally James took a suck or two each time I had my eyes in another direction. I finally gave them all to Vanette. Bruce turned his face to the window and started meowing quite loudly. Under my breath I threatened him with instant removal.

Although Bruce's other stims have changed over the months, he has always loved to meow, especially in public. When he first came, he would constantly pull his shirt down over his shoulder to kiss himself. He would also look at his elbow, flicking it up and down, in and out of his eye range, or sit staring at his thumb. We still see these stims, but much less frequently. Lately he has acquired another, irritating one: vocalized breathing, almost panting, into his palm cupped in front of his mouth.

Sanford was bewildered by all this confusion, poor guy, but actually the meal went well. The toddlers across the aisle were much louder and more unruly than we were.

On the train and bus I had charge of Bruce and James, both of them veterans of public transportation. They were quiet and attentive to the scenery. Toward the very end James got a bit restive, so I let him sneak a flap with the strap of my backpack.

Once at the zoo the three of us were still together. With all the noisy distractions, it was hard to get them to focus on anything. I waited until we were directly in front of a cage, then I turned their heads toward the animal. That way I could *feel* that they saw, especially James, by the tension in their bodies. I signed "milk" by the cows and "eggs" by the chickens for James's hungry interests; I called the jaguars and lions "big kitty cats" for Bruce. In front of the monkey cage, I asked James what they were doing. He signed, correctly, "sleeping."

The trip home was, for the most part, uneventful. On the bus Bruce perched on Sanford's lap and repeatedly sang out "I—wan'—big—Mac!" in his most plaintive, highly pitched voice, much to the other passengers' amusement and Sanford's embarrassment.

Then on the train, Lincoln sat next to a well-built, rather tough-looking young black man. Lincoln started bouncing around in his seat, muttering to himself, shadow-boxing—a horribly mean and utterly feigned look on his face. The black guy was getting more and more nervous by the minute and tried to fade into the window. I watched in enjoyment until finally I offered Lincoln a stick of gum, thereby letting his seatmate know that someone was accompanying the "mad boxer." Wouldn't he be surprised if he could see Lincoln at home—sucking his thumb!

Sunday

What a contrast to yesterday's sunny excursion! It rained the whole day, so time for housecleaning was at hand. Sanford was worried about the sump pump in the houseparent's apartment (I didn't blame him; it often didn't work); Vanette was full of complaints. I worked hard to try and keep myself on task; it is so easy to become lethargic on days like these. I went from child to child, charting each on a task they needed to do. Again, I made sure James did a lion's share—he changed his sheets, did a wash, folded towels, vacuumed, and set the table for lunch.

Bruce was on a home visit, so with both him and Sylvester gone, the house seemed unusually quiet, and cozy because of the rain.

Saturday

Bruce had been the big news of the preceding week. What we had thought last weekend was a sun rash turned out to be something else—an accompaniment to strep throat. The doctor put him on ampicillin, and Bruce suffered a severe allergic reaction to it. His face swelled up, the skin all over his body became mottled and itchy, he had a fever and difficulty in breathing. One scary night his mother had to take him to the emergency room for a shot of adrenalin. And if that crisis weren't enough, one night he bit off an entire fingernail in his sleep, possibly during a seizure. Of necessity the whole finger is now swathed in a bandage.

Poor Bruce! The last role in the world he needs to play is the invalid one, and he falls into it like a charm. Naturally with that finger he cannot pull on his slightly shrunken socks by himself, or tuck his sheets under his mattress. He sits, quite relaxed, waiting for the help which he knows is forthcoming. I instantly saw how this role must have been played out during all his years at home before he came here: sit quietly while Mama dresses him. How much easier than waiting him out, till he does it himself, and how unavoidable in a household which could not function if it had to run on "autistic time."

Vanette and Sanford are not yet imbued enough with the independent spirit, either. At Sanford's request, Vanette had made a whole platter of French toast and bacon by the time I got downstairs with the little guys. Neutral as I try to remain, I had to protest, especially when Vanette commented that everyone ate much more when we all sat down at the same time.

"But you see, they're supposed to be learning cooking skills. Every one of these guys can make their own French toast."

"But it's so chaotic when they cook."

"So what?"

"Well . . . they do that all week."

"No, they eat cold cereal. They're in a rush for school."

"Well," Sanford compromised, "Maybe each weekend a different boy can help cook breakfast."

The trouble is, the staff is too emotionally involved with food. Besides, I hate to see the philosophy of the home change into simple maintenance from our original goal of creatively challenging the boys. Dolores was splendid for that very reason; she always found the status quo of the boys boring, and had the energy to try to change it for the better.

Bruce's mother came to pick him up for a day visit; Mack's grandmother and father came to take him out for lunch. I spent a lot of time talking with them all. The parents have more contact with the weekend staff than they do with the daily staff, aside from the house manager, and on Saturdays and Sundays till 2:30, I am the only familiar face, the sole holdover from the original staff. I can imagine how this turnover is worrisome to them; I can certainly see relief return to their faces as we talk. They only want to make sure their children are loved.

Mack's eighty-year-old grandma waited at the car while his father brought him back after lunch. "Grandma, I can't do without my hug!" I shouted at her and ran down the sidewalk. She grinned and turned to give me a big hug and kiss. Grandma was worried about Mack's speech. He didn't seem to talk too much during lunch, she said, but perhaps he was feeling the heat. I tried to reassure her. When he said one or two words, we always requested he combine them into a full sentence, and we could always get one. That's the tactic she had used, she said. She is a fantastic grandma. Too bad she can't run faster, we could give her a job!

Mack has, in fact, made a lot of progress in speech since he has been in the group home. Up until he was five years old, he was mute, but had acquired a 120-word vocabulary in sign language. When he did begin to speak, he completely stopped signing. He had also flapped, like James, but gave it up spontaneously, too.

Bruce's mother had been through hell this past week and seemed relieved to see him looking so much better. She refuses to believe he bit his own nail off, because he's never been a nail-biter. She also said that when coming back from a home visit last weekend, tears filled his eyes and he whispered, "miss Dolores." This from a child supposedly unable to form relationships! The staff cannot help but be aware of the effect of staff turnover on the boys' behavior. I am not sure we are all as aware of the effect on their psyches, of which there may be fewer, quieter signs.

For a while Lincoln and I were home entirely by ourselves. He had earned some free time and chose to spend it watching television. I went into the kitchen to clean, but I didn't like it. It was too damn normal. So after a few minutes I went in and asked Lincoln if he could please come unload the dishwasher for me. Sure, he said. So we worked together and talked, and I felt pretty good about my use of the time we had alone. Lincoln does not have very good communication skills and has a hard time stringing together his questions and comments into a coherent conversation. In his months of living at the home, however, he too has made a tremendous improvement—due to the fact that all the staff make a consistent effort to talk with him.

Then Sylvester entered the picture. He and James and Sanford had been at the park; now Sylvester's job was to set the table for lunch, and I wanted Lincoln to prepare a can of soup. So the three of us were in the kitchen. Sylvester started in with his silliness, grabbing my hands, pinching them, teasing he would hurt me. Lincoln joined in, imitating everything Sylvester did in both words and deed—except Lincoln could really hurt because he has no sense of his strength, especially when he gets carried away in competing with Sylvester.

I tried to ignore Lincoln, because it was impossible for me to deal physically with both of them together, and led Sylvester to the table. I sat on the bench holding his arms, while he giggled and pinched my wrists. Lincoln sat on the other side of the table, reaching over repeatedly to clout me on the back.

Meanwhile Sanford was on the phone with Lucy, the house manager, having, as far as I could tell, a polite but meaningless conversation compared with my situation. After a few more clouts, I lost my patience and shouted, "Sanford, will you *hang up* the phone!" He hung up and took Lincoln into the living room. When he returned, I apologized.

Sanford's neurosis appears to be the telephone.

Sunday

A productive morning: I was able to go fairly smoothly from child to child, task to task, clipboard in hand.

Bruce was climbing again. He repeatedly entered the director's office and climbed atop the desks and file cabinets. He walked on the backs of the couches. Vanette had put a load of laundry in the washer with him; then I went with him to put it in the dryer. He stood gazing into the open washer and tried to walk away, only to have my hand fall on his shoulder after a step or so.

"Get your clothes out, Bruce."

"Bend over, Bruce."

"Put your hand in the machine, Bruce."

It took many minutes of prompting and catching him to get the whole load into his basket. Then he closed the lid and attempted to set the dial and turn the empty washer on—a correct action, but in the wrong sequence.

After lunch, he and I again went in the basement to empty the dryer. He stood there, rubbing his finger back and forth along his tongue. I didn't feel like prompting him; I leaned against the dryer and sang while I waited, a Rod Stewart song with misplaced words. "You're in my heart, you're in my soul, you'll be my lover should I grow old; la la la LA, la la la LA, you're . . . in . . . my . . . *soul.*"

Well, I sang this over several times, feeling a bit

like Winnie the Pooh humming a hum to little Piglet. Suddenly Bruce looked up at me, alert and focused, and sang my final phrase, in perfect tune: "You're in my . . . *choul!*"

I laughed and we sang together. In a minute he began to pitch the clothes from the dryer into his basket. The song certainly perked him up. Together we carried the clothes upstairs into the living room. I wasn't going to ask him to do any more work, but he picked one of his shirts out and folded it. I ran for his clipboard.

He folded his whole load, with minimal prompting, while distractions abounded around us. I didn't have him turn things right-side out, because of his bandage, and he balked at matching and folding socks together, but he remained, in staff jargon, extremely "available" for almost forty-five minutes.

When he had finished, he sat down in a chair and took his shoes off. I told him he had to put his shoes back on, because it was almost time to go on the afternoon outing. He erupted into a tantrum, screaming and pulling my hair. I took him into the kitchen because it was quieter there; I sat him on the bench and said that when he was calm, he could put his shoes on. He jumped up, pulling the tablecloth off the table and trying to rip a ceramic sculpture off the wall. When I caught him, he grabbed my hair.

I sat holding his hands, my legs scissoring his.

"Let go? Ready to go?"

"When you're calm, I'll let you go."

"Let go?"

"Are you going to put on your shoes?"

"Yes."

"Okay."

I let him go. He threw the shoes down and grabbed for the tablecloth again, but I caught him first. We went back and forth for maybe twenty minutes, wearing each other out. Since it's unproductive to get angry at Bruce during a tantrum, you need the patience of a saint. Plus he might be seizing. I gave him chance after chance to sit calmly and put on his shoes. Finally he complied.

"I want need help!" (a favorite, if ungrammatical, request).

"You put them on; I'll tie them."

With that crisis over, I led him by the hand back to the living room. We sat together in a chair and I read him a long boring book about boats. His eyes got heavier and heavier as he relaxed in my arms.

"Do you want to lie down?"

"Yes."

I found that hard to believe, but he lay down on the couch and I covered him with a freshly washed sheet. A second later he was sound asleep. He'd had a rough couple of hours.

Saturday

Since Lincoln's mother got punched during his last home visit, the new plan is for her to visit him at the group home on Saturday mornings. If she feels safe enough, then, she can take him out for lunch. Today, however, she was full of goodwill and enthusiasm, ready to take Lincoln out for an excursion as soon as she arrived.

"Going to see any Lawn-Boys?" he asked her by way of greeting.

"Yes, we'll go see Lawn-Boys."

Her idea of an excursion is to go to the shopping mall and let Lincoln drool over the lawnmowers and vacuum cleaners. So they left. Sooner than I had expected, they returned. She had a bag from McDonalds and he had a big toy box of some kind. They went upstairs to have lunch together in privacy. Before she followed Lincoln up, she whispered to me that he was beginning to get nervous at the mall, so she brought him back early.

After the rest of us had finished lunch, Sanford wondered if Lincoln's mother would like to come down and bake chocolate chip cookies with her son. I ventured my personal opinion—no. I reasoned she wouldn't feel comfortable expanding her role in the home; she had always stayed with Lincoln upstairs, unobserved, till the Big Macs were gone, then she had left.

As happens with great regularity, I was wrong. She accepted Sanford's suggestion and came into the kitchen with Lincoln. However, she stipulated that she would sit and watch Sanford and Lincoln because she could not bake at all, and these cookies were to be made from scratch, not a mix.

There was hardly enough "scratch" to make them, anyway, because James repeatedly snitched the chips. And Sanford melted the butter instead of creaming it with the sugar. But everyone persevered, and Lincoln's mother was impressed enough to volunteer to bring a brownie mix next time.

I looked at the toy she had bought Lincoln. It

was a green inflatable half-man, half-monster, a hideous thing—reduced from $22 to $7, presumably because most people found it hideous, too. Lincoln tinkered with its air valve and sucked its extremities in lieu of his thumb.

Sunday

Today's excursion was a visit to a German old people's home which was having its annual fair. Shortly before lunch we trooped off, carrying our own fried chicken and peaches picnic. The home itself was set far back from the street, fronted by an enormous lawn now filled with various booths, concession stands, and picnic tables.

We sat and ate, the kids in a good mood because they loved the chicken. James was an ear-to-ear smear of grease, and Bruce was eating so greedily he was totally indifferent to the appearance of an erstwhile hero, Ronald McDonald.

Afterward we split up. I took Mack to see the dunking booth, where people lined up to throw balls at a lever which submerged some presumably well-known local personage in cold water. Certainly he got dunked, but not as often as if his "attackers" had been sober. It made for a merry scene, and Mack joined right in. He thought it was great. In fact, several times he tried to dash up to the booth: "Mack go in water, too!"

He was reluctant to leave, but finally I got him steered over to the pony ride, where Sanford was waiting in line with James and Bruce. All the boys gave signals of assent when asked if they wanted to ride. I was surprised, especially at Mack, who had a fear of animals, and envisioned either him or Bruce tantrumming in mid-ride and causing a stampede.

Bruce got to the head of the line without changing his mind, so I asked for a helper to lead the pony while I walked alongside. I had no trouble at all with Bruce, who clutched the reins and closed his eyes, but plenty with the pony, who was so fat he kept squashing me against the guardrail.

"Wave to Sanford, Bruce!" Bruce managed to unsqueeze his eyes for a quick wave, and then attended to the reins again. I was sorry we didn't have a camera; if only his mother could see him now, I thought.

Sanford escorted James around, and then Mack. James was ecstatic, trying to flap the pony's mane. Mack was hesitant, then happy. Sanford even got him to pet the pony!

The German band was just starting up, so we all went over and got front-row seats. Bruce sat quietly and rocked in time to the polkas and drinking songs; James climbed in Sanford's lap to listen. Mack kept telling me he was going on the pony ride again. Granted he has a terrific memory for schedules, but he can really drive you crazy, perseverating on them.

Suddenly, when I relaxed my vigilance with the kids and looked around, tears came into my eyes: all these old German people listening to music from a yesteryear life. Two women danced in front of us, carefully supporting each other's fragile bones. And our boys seemed so in contrast, beginning their lives, but in their own way just as fragile and even more vulnerable.

Vanette had already gone home with Rod. Another member of the staff whispered in my ear as she went, "Vanette just can't handle geriatrics." I stopped in to say good-bye to the two of them when I went back for my bike. They were sitting on the couch, and Vanette told Rod to give me a hug good-bye. He rushed at me and gave me a kiss on the lips!

He has been so sweet and in control of himself these past few weeks. I have been able to gain a lot of confidence in working with him. Unfortunately Vanette is quitting at the end of the summer, and the transition time with her replacement, however capable that person may turn out to be, will be rough for Rod—as all staff turnovers are for all the boys.

Friday

I worked the 2:00 to 10:00 P.M. shift today, the final day of the kids' summer recreation program. They came off the bus with their paperwork, various party knickknacks, and, hidden but soon discovered, packages of red licorice sticks. They got permission to eat them, but not from me; all I could think of was red for artificial flavor, licorice for sugar. Diet is another object of controversy among the staff. For most of them, a "normalizing" environment includes normally processed and refined junk food; the minority, principally Dolores and I, waged ongoing battles to replace, for example, white bread with whole grain. After Dolores left, the normalizing faction took control.

Sanford divided up the kids among the staff to go on a predinner walk to McDonalds. I got Lincoln, along with the question of whether I felt comfortable alone with him. He has been acting out more than usual lately.

"Sure," I replied. "Linc's my buddy."

I went upstairs to get him, where he had been sent to change his shirt.

"Hurry up, Lincoln. We're going out, you and I."

"Just us?"

He got a big grin on his face, which quickly turned hostile when I said yes, we were going out for a snack.

"Let's not sit by the others, okay? I don't wanna sit by anyone else."

"Okay, okay, just change your shirt. You go out with me, you have to be clean."

He continued to swing between being happy and being crabby. He was particularly hostile toward the two male staff members. As I promised, we sat at a separate table at McDonalds, while he inhaled a sundae (more sugar) and did his head-turning-to-look-behind-him stim.

Next we went to the supermarket. I had forgotten to bring the shopping list, so we couldn't do it the proper way. Lincoln manned the cart up and down the aisles while I tried to remember what to buy.

I did remember that bacon was on the list, and while I looked over the packages Lincoln insisted on squeezing the hotdogs. When we got to the dairy case, he insisted on squeezing the cheese while I checked the eggs. Sylvester had been the only boy I had taken here before, so Lincoln was a new experience.

We got home before everyone else, so after Lincoln put away the groceries I asked him to load the dishwasher while I washed the counters. The kitchen would be clean to start dinner. He was very slow-moving and quiet. I respected his silence, something I don't do very often, as we worked together.

Later in the evening he got rambunctious, giving Sanford a hard time. Upstairs putting Bruce and James to bed, I could hear him screaming and moaning that he wanted to watch television downstairs. (A few minutes before, when I had still been there, he hadn't been at all interested in the program.) Sanford finally got him upstairs, in his room, and said that when he was quiet, he could come out and talk with him or watch television. Lincoln moaned a while, then came out and plopped in a chair. He answered all Sanford's attempts at conversation with a "I dunno," muttered around the thumb in his mouth.

He did ask Sanford if he could talk with me for a little bit. Sanford said yes, when I was done with the other boys. Well, it took me a while, not with Bruce who had fallen asleep quickly, but with James. I wanted to sit guard until he was asleep, too, so he wouldn't hop up and flap all Bruce's pajamas into colorful twirled ropes. For a long time he lay and sang a beautiful la-la-la song, till he slept.

Lincoln waited. He just wanted to talk about Lawn-Boys and the schedule for the weekend. I tucked him in and kissed him goodnight. For Lincoln, every male staff member seemed a father to rebel against; every female, a tender touch.

Saturday

When several staff members go to the park with several of the kids, or even when one takes several kids, it is clear what we are: an abnormally extended family. But when we are one-on-one, we look like a father or mother taking their child on a little outing. This morning James and I went to the park in such a guise.

We made a wierd mother/son duo. James had been crabby all morning, grumpy and whining. He had constantly wanted his ribs and back scratched, leading me to the couch and lifting his shirt. I did it for a while, in between his tasks, but he was being really insistent about this basically boring and unproductive stim. Finally I explained to him that enough was enough and stopped scratching. He threw a tantrum.

I ignored it. When he had quieted down, I told him we were going to the park in a few minutes, so he should find his shoes and put them on. He began another tantrum. Sanford came in at that point.

"If he doesn't want to go, he can stay with me; you can take somebody else."

"Sanford, I'm not *giving* him a choice. Of course, he'd rather stay home; that's not the point."

"Oh."

James continued to complain during the entire hot walk to the park. I steadfastly ignored him, except to take his hand in dangerous places, which further annoyed him. By the time we got there, I was annoyed, too.

The only other people there were a Hispanic

woman and her two little daughters. Despite the heat and grubbiness of the playground, she was wearing designer jeans and high heels, and her daughters had on party dresses and hair ribbons. Here came James toward their group—clapping his hands, kicking his heels up behind him, but in noisy, whining complaint, not in happiness. The woman looked at me with a questioning, mother-to-mother look. I turned away from her look when, I suppose, I should have given her a return smile and a condensed lecture on autism: good community relations, but I wasn't in the mood.

James went down the slide, kneeling in the dirt at the bottom and spraying it with his hands. At least he was quiet. After he did that for a while, he started trotting toward the swings. He had to pass the girls to get there, so I took after him at a dead run, in case he decided to lay hold of their hair. (He does have the habit of pulling hair, two handfuls at a time, even of strange children out in public, especially if they are littler than he.) He barely looked at them, but the mother gave me a warning look.

The swinging didn't last long, then he slid back into the dirt, periodically letting out a howl, to which I replied, "Knock it off!" By now, the mother was regarding us as exhibits: what a crazy kid, what an awful mother.

Like everyone else in the home, I am so used to our kids' behaviors that it is easy to forget how bizarre they appear to outsiders. A staff member (who has since quit) told me how her boyfriend came to pick her up one night, and she invited him right in. After all, she had told him how great "her" kids were. Well, it was a particularly wild night, after shower but before bedtime. The kids were all in various stages of being pajamaed, all climbing the walls . . . or the couches, or the tables. She saw her friend's mouth drop, and turned around to view the scene freshly, through his eyes. She burst out laughing.

"*This* is where you *work!*" was his flabbergasted comment.

It was time for James and me to go home for lunch. I told him so, and that he should get a drink of water at the fountain on the way. For the first time in a few hours, he grinned. As we walked together across the playground, the mother called out to me, "Do you have the time?" I told her and smiled, belatedly. I don't think she cared at all what time it was; I think she just wanted to elicit some normal response.

Sunday

This morning I got the little guys doing some tasks they used to do, but which have somehow disappeared from the weekend schedule. So James, first of all, washed the living-room windows and the bathroom mirrors. I had to watch him every second, or he would spray the cleaner in his mouth, or lick the drops off the glass, or chew on the rag. He was pretty lazy, too, about rubbing the glass. He certainly gave it more of a lick than a polish. However, I did notice he could look at the arrow on the sprayer to check what direction the liquid would come out. That is progress.

James's last evaluation report noted that he tends to learn exactly what he is taught—nothing more, nothing less. Consequently, he depends quite heavily on an adult prompt or cajole to carry him from one task to the other. We should, the report says, be helping him to gain more initiative, so he does not have to be prodded throughout his whole day's activities. The report also noted that James frequently uses sign language under the table or while walking away from staff and then tantrums when his needs aren't met. Suggested remedies were instituting a communication card system and making James get the staff's attention before signing.

Sanford has been working on the latter: he has been teaching him to tap him on the shoulder (James scratches him instead, naturally) or to vocalize "Sa" to get his attention. Working out a comm-card system, however, is meeting with delays of a mysterious nature. I'm all for it.

Bruce was going home for the day, but I wanted him to do a little work before he left. I had him dust with a spray wax, which he hasn't done in several months. He did all right, with only a few screams, but of course I had to lead him from one piece of furniture to another, and start his hand moving the rag.

I also did laundry with Bruce. As always, I am amazed by his memorization of sequences, how he seemingly learns pieces without ever getting a sense of the whole, for instance, turning dirty clothes into clean, dry ones. Staring at a basket of wet clothes, he will not know whether to put them in the washer or the dryer.

Saturday

Today the schedule was changed around a bit; the outing was moved up to mid-morning. It was decided Bruce should stay home with me because he has been suffering from an upset stomach on and off for the past week. Poor Bruce seems to have one trouble after another. When I woke him this morning, he was stuffy and congested as well.

The outing was chosen by Lincoln, so naturally when the time came, he decided he didn't want to go. I felt as if I had an invisible crowbar at the front door, trying to wedge them out before somebody "blew." All transitions are hard for the kids: indoors to out, outdoors to in.

At last Bruce and I had the house to ourselves. I wanted to mix work with quieter activities, so Bruce would have a basically restful day. I started washing dishes and asked Bruce to clean the table. I gave him a wet cloth; he started rubbing one spot on a placemat. I then got engrossed in my own thoughts, looking up every now and then to encourage him. Then there was a phone call. When I finished, Bruce had moved his hand, but was still cleaning the same placemat.

I figured it was time to move on. We began on his laundry. The kids are all going to camp for two weeks Monday, so everyone will need clean clothes. He got his basket willingly enough, but tried to negotiate the two flights of stairs to the basement with his eyes closed. I had to prompt him through the rest of the task.

Then we sat in the living room and I turned on

the radio. Bruce sat quietly on the couch, seemingly content; he loves to listen to music. In a few minutes, however, he burst out crying. I asked him what the matter was.

"Go home?" he whispered through his tears.

"You're going home tomorrow, Bruce. Tomorrow."

It was so hard to comfort him. He stopped crying, but slowly became more and more unavailable. Sometimes not looking at him at all helps; now I decided to try the opposite. I stared at him fixedly, continuously, and when he looked back at me, I said nothing but smiled at him in a relaxed way. When he noticed my intense looking, at first it only made him look at me more often. After a while he began to have a more relaxed expression when he returned my looks. He came to sit in my lap with a *TV Guide* he had picked off the bookshelf.

Since that choice offered no good reading possibilities, I just continued smiling at him. Finally he looked at the advertisement on the back of the magazine, looked at me with a small smile, and said, "I want a cigarette!"

James's ninth birthday comes during camp week, so family friends chose tonight to invite him for dinner and a party. The job fell to me to get him showered and dressed. Showering was easy, because James loves water; dressing was harder because all his clothes were dirty. Even the clean ones in his drawers were either hopelessly stained or hopelessly small. James himself picked out his bathing suit and started to put it on. I realized that he thought he was going to his parents' home for a swim in their pool.

"No, James, you're not going home. You're going to the Duncans.'"

He began to tantrum—he loves to swim—but I quickly subdued him. The poor kid then had to put on and take off pants and shirts umpteen times while I tried to put together an outfit fairly clean and somewhat fancy. After all, it *was* a party. I hated this job because my taste in clothing never matches that of the other staff members, and I always get hollered at for my choices. Finally it was settled: new blue jogging shorts, risky because they posed a great temptation for James's busy fingers, and a clean tee-shirt I had found in the bottom of his drawer with the words "Super Jock" on it.

I forestalled criticism by announcing I had no other choice. Then the problem was keeping James out of the kitchen, where hamburgers and french fries were sizzling. I couldn't seem to make him understand he couldn't have two dinners.

At last the doorbell rang: Mr. Duncan and his college-age daughter Alice, an old caretaker of James. They were quite happy to see each other. As I watched them walk hand-in-hand down the front sidewalk, I had to laugh: Alice, too, was wearing blue jogging shorts and a red tee-shirt.

Sunday

The house was pretty empty again today. There were three staff people for two kids, James and Rod. The others were all home, or slated to leave soon: Lincoln with his father, Bruce with all his relatives because today is *his* birthday, Sylvester home all weekend, and Mack home, too, for the day.

Today is a big milestone for Mack, his first home

visit since moving here. His family has taken him out for the day, but never home. Yesterday and this morning we primed him, so he knew when and where he was going, and that he was coming back to sleep and going to camp tomorrow.

"Ride horsies at camp."

"Yes, Mack."

"And go swimming."

"Yes, Mack. And I'll see you when you get back from camp."

His mother and sister arrived to fetch him. They were both happily nervous, but Mack had no such ambiguity of feeling: his whole body was smiling.

I hugged and kissed him good-bye. "Bye Mack. See you later."

"See you, Mack get back from camp," he corrected as he walked off between his mom and his twin, holding hands with both.

Afterward

Six months after the final journal entry, a new child, Justin, has moved into the home. He is ten years old, weighs barely fifty pounds. Food, as his psychological work-up states, "is not reinforcing to Justin." He needs a thousand prompts to get him through a meal. One morning I spent an hour and a half coaxing him to eat a slice of bread with peanut butter. He almost finished it, between sips from my coffee cup. His speech is mostly echolalic, and very speeded-up, lilting, so that it sounds like a special Japanese autistic language. He can be physically very affectionate and makes excellent, alert eye contact with his brown Mediterranean eyes. He is an extremely beautiful child.

Of greatest interest to me is Justin's stim. He makes designs of anything with texture or nap, like the pile lining of his coat or the bodies of his huge stuffed animals. Chattering away in his unique "jay-bird" style, he sits and pushes the fur this way and that. If not distracted, his chattering may increase in volume and aggravated tone until he jumps up in a frenzy, slamming doors and scratching people. (Scratching is an appropriate mode of aggression for him.) Possibly he gets frustrated in his attempts at perfection in his work. He also likes to make designs with Etch-a-Sketch—a staircase is a favorite design, which he will verbally label as "stairs"—but here again, he can get frustrated. His design work seemingly is a pleasure/pain mixture: the artist's dilemma.

Here is a child who is very sensitive to skin pressure—he manifests this in other ways, too, such as dislike of showering water, the feel of a toothbrush against his teeth, and anything but nylon socks on his feet—and who is also very sensitive to pattern.

This newest autistic friend presents an interesting synthesis of a characteristic I have noted among all the boys, although expressed in different modes: obsession with order. For Rod, a low-functioning child, this order is very literal. He continually straightens shoes in closets, adjusts furniture, closes doors, gathers dishtowels and washrags to stuff back into the drawer (be they wet or dry), and so on. For James, order is abstracted into a higher level of structure; he cares very little for content, he is watching edges, shadows, patterns on the wall. Likewise, his repertoire of flapping/jumping/

kicking movement is not random; it is extremely ordered and rhythmical movement.

"Rhythm is the great organizer. Habits of accent form to hold an organism together, patterns of rhythmical shape lend sense and sensibility to life." So writes Doris Humphrey in *The Art of Making Dances*; James is nothing if not a dancer. Of course, the point is that James's abstractions make him even more handicapped and disadvantaged than Rod, because society at least values a tidy closet.

Principally because his speech progress was so rapid, Mack, on the other hand, has not remained quite as incomprehensible as James. From the first, he was fascinated with spaces inside and spaces behind—radiators, furniture, vacuum hoses. He was constantly stuffing little toys and bits of garbage in these hard-to-reach places. It never occurred to me that he was trying to get his own body in the same places as I watched him on hands and knees in front of a radiator. But one day he told me, "Mack go in too," while poking a piece of dirt inside the vacuum hose. I explained to him about his body size. He didn't respond, but from then on we had similar conversations in similar situations, and because his receptive vocabulary was increasing, he was able to understand.

Tunnels became a new preoccupation, born of train travels around the city. He was initially terrified, but then grew to love them. Finally he began pretending that the two flights of stairs down to the basement comprised a tunnel, which the area certainly does resemble. He talked of trains going through this tunnel and expressed a desire to sleep there, all with the clear apperception that he was pretending. But he had found a space large enough for his body to move in and out of. His latest imaginary addition to this tunnel is another stairway up through the ceiling. When I asked him where he wanted these stairs to go, he replied, "Go to a department store, buy candy!"

Even his habit of running along baseboards inside the house and a row of bushes outside the house became more intelligible. To us they are baseboards and bushes; to him they are lines, the boundaries of ins and outs.

I am almost sure that if James could talk, he would express the same concern with ins and outs and straight lines. Only recently I observed James climb up on top of a radiator cover and stretch up and up along the wall as if to reach the line where wall and ceiling meet. My initial reaction was to tell him to get down, but his expression and behavior were so full of intention, I didn't. After a few such stretches, he calmly got down and continued making his bed. I was reminded of a cat who jumps from chair top to shelf, not content until it has reached the highest accessible point in the room.

Mack's interest in structural patterns has, logically enough, shifted from physical objects toward language. Again, it took me a while to sense what this new interest meant. One day he kept perseverating on the difference between "hot" and "cold," and "right" and "wrong." I thought he was just looking for an argument (which he loves to do) when, in the shower, he kept judging the water "too–oo hot" and then, at the most minute adjustment, "too–oo cold." While looking at my notes for that day, I suddenly realized how concern with opposites is interest in verbal structure, differing only in content from in and out of tunnels, real or pretend. He had merely shifted to another hierarchy of thought.

From then on, I paid special attention to his language. The expression of time structure is also important to Mack. He learned the names of the days of the week and loved to recite them; then he progressed to "yesterday" and "tomorrow" and could accurately correlate events with them, usually school days versus nonschool days, or breakfast menus. His latest achievement along this line has been the correlation of three successive days with three favorite brands of cereal. He said, slowly, with much labor and deliberation: "Wednesday, Puffed Rice; Thursday, Golden Grahams; Friday, Honey, Nuts 'n Raisin." Then he looked at me with justifiable pride. He had matched two three-part sequences in what was for him a very long sentence.

He learned his colors well, too, and then began matching them up. One morning it took him thirty minutes to brush his teeth, because the toothpaste was a new color, green, like his pants. He began inventing all new manner of toothpastes to match all his articles of clothing. That evening he commented that his toothbrush was orange and announced that he wanted a "grapefruit toothbrush!" Now he was *playing* with the structure, another level yet.

Again, he told me I had on "blue pants."

"Yes," I replied. "Blue jeans."

He gazed at me a second, and then, recalling the

day's staffing schedule, said mischievously, "Blue Gene come tonight!"

‡‡

Overall, the pictures drawn of the boys may seem overly bizarre to anyone who is not familiar with this type of child. In a way, however, this criticism is accurate, because my accounts are inevitably biased by time and place. I never saw the boys in their classrooms, and although the houseparents were in close contact with the teachers and a log notebook went back and forth between the school and the home on a daily basis, information about the boys' academic progress rarely filtered down to part-time, weekend staff. I do know that even James had been taught to scrawl out the letters of his name, and that the rest of the boys were learning, however slowly, to read. By no means all autistic children are retarded to the same degree, or even at all; the trick, of course, is to *reach* them. Creative teaching methods and appropriate testing techniques are two more challenges to those interested in making a contribution.

Certainly it is difficult for me, personally, to assess the value of my work in the group home. Undeniably I learned more from them than they did from me, partly because I was only one of many staff members, partly, as mentioned earlier, because of my changed ideas about the prognosis for an autistic child. With Karen I could say, with at least some justification: "See, she's laughing! I helped her do that!"; with the boys, progress was infinitely less tangible. I am not nearly as satisfied with the thought that I taught James to wax a coffee table. I do feel good that there were moments when each of them needed comfort, or help, or direction, and I was able to be there to give it to them.

How often I reminded myself that if the moment is all there is for any of us, how much more true for children who, in a sense, live outside of time.

Conclusion

After working with this admittedly small sample of autistic children in two very different milieus, there are very few conclusions I feel confident in drawing from my experience. One would certainly have to be agreement with the current behavioral description of the syndrome. Whether the child is under- or over-active, he or she is recognizably autistic. The only characteristic I find questionable is the one probably most popularly associated with autism—the inability to form appropriate relationships with other people. If we view the term "appropriate" simply as a societal value judgement, I think it is clear that these children can and do form strong bonds of attachment.

No more than anyone else, obviously, do I know what autism is or what causes it. I have at times found the idea appealing that there might be two kinds of autism, one caused by an organic dysfunction, the other caused environmentally, that have identical behavioral symptoms. This idea was triggered by an experience working with a group of mentally retarded women, whose similarity to one another was, for me, a source of surprise. One young woman, for example, had suffered retardation as a result of phenylketonuria (PKU), an enzyme-deficiency disease now correctable through diet if diagnosed at birth; one woman had had an extremely abusive and deprived childhood; one woman's brain had not had enough oxygen at birth (fetal anoxia). But *behaviorally* you could not distinguish one woman from the other; they all had both emotional and physical problems. I had to read their case histories to sort out the causes. There were no neat and tidy checklists of behavioral descriptions to distinguish organic damage from deprivation of bonding, or whatever.

Two points about this realization impressed me very deeply: first, that if you did enough terrible things to an initially normal infant or child you could, for all outward appearances, mimic perfectly an organic condition; and second, that in dealing with these people *right now*, the etiology of their deficits is not very important. Both these insights seem applicable to autistic children.

An appealing idea, however, does not have to be correct; this one may be attractive simply because it lets everyone, in a sense, be correct. But, in fact, no theory has proved satisfactory (which is why there are so many), and none has generated very satisfactory therapies, either.

Currently the pendulum is swinging, ever so slightly, back toward at least looking at emotional causes. Niko Tinbergen, a pioneer in ethology, has, along with his wife Elisabeth, been looking at autistic children with eyes which have been acutely observing animals for years (*Autistic Children: New Hope for a Cure*, 1983). They see autism, even its accompanying seizures, as resulting from a motivational conflict between approach and avoidance tendencies, stemming from an initial failure of bonding, particularly with the mother. As therapy, they advocate the work of Dr. Martha Welch, whose technique consists of daily mother/child holding sessions. With the somewhat jaundiced view of someone who has spent a lot of time holding autistic children, I am dubious that this technique is a cure-all. On the other hand, what handicapped child would *not* benefit from such an intense expression of love, a love which may be quite strained by the handicap itself.

The value in using an ethological approach lies, I think, in its stress upon *observing* the child, and observing without, at least in the beginning, labeling or judging. This patient observation, a skill rarely taught or valued these days, leads one to an intimate awareness of the other, and consequently of the other's needs. If I want to know how best I can help this child, I must not rush in with my ready-made theories and answers; I must first *see* this child. It sounds very simple; it is not.

I am not saying that it does not really matter what autism finally turns out to be. I am saying that while the professionals fill up journals with their brain studies and conditioning techniques, many of them with contradictory results, those directly caring for autistic children, let alone the children themselves, do not have time to wait for *the* definitive answer. These workers may even be crippling the child further by adhering to one or another dogma, which inevitably filters or distorts reality.

If we view autism solely as an organic dysfunction, we are less likely to help autistic children with their emotional or psychic problems. The inability to communicate at all or very well with the people in their environment clearly has to result in emotional problems, whatever the root cause of the deficit. (Witness James as a good example.) All children, damaged in some way or not, have an active psychic life which needs nurturing.

If, on the other hand, we view autism solely as an emotional problem, we waste time and energy looking for the proper place to lay the guilt; we may stress the child further by imputing to him normal intellectual and cognitive powers which, in fact, he may not have, or may have been lost forever.

I will leave the final words to anthropologist Gregory Bateson, because they are especially meaningful to those of us who work with children:

> *The fact of our imperfect understanding should not be allowed to feed our anxiety and so increase the need to control. Rather, our studies could be inspired by a more ancient, but today less honored motive: a curiosity about the world of which we are a part. The rewards of such work are not power, but beauty.**

*David Lipset, *Gregory Bateson: The Legacy of a Scientist* (Englewood Cliffs, N.J.: Prentice-Hall, 1980).

Suggestions for Further Reading

The following list is a short selection from the autism literature. It is a totally biased sample: all are books I have read and found valuable.

Bettelheim, Bruno. *The Empty Fortress: Infantile Autism and the Birth of the Self.* New York: Free Press, 1967.

———. *A Home for the Heart.* New York: Knopf, 1974.

However maligned by the autistic community, the depth of Bettelheim's commitment to children remains an inspiration.

Park, Clara Claiborne. *The Siege: The First Eight Years of an Autistic Child (With an Epilogue, Fifteen Years Later).* Boston: Little, Brown, 1982.

Of all the narratives written by parents of autistic children, this one is my favorite.

Selfe, Lorna. *Nadia: A Case of Extraordinary Drawing Ability in an Autistic Child.* London: Academic Press, 1977.

Nadia's drawings are extraordinarily beautiful and an exception to the developmental sequence shown by other children, normal or abnormal, in their art. Nadia apparently skipped all the steps and began at the top.

Shattuck, Roger. *The Forbidden Experiment: The Story of the Wild Boy of Aveyron.* New York: Farrar, Straus & Giroux, 1980.

After I read about Victor, I became convinced he

was autistic, although Shattuck says no. In a related book, Harlan Lane and Richard Pillard (*The Wild Boy of Burundi: A Study of an Outcast Child* [New York: Random House, 1978]) go to Africa, excited by the prospect of finding a modern-day Wild Boy—only to find Balthazar, a classically autistic child. They are disappointed.

Tinbergen, Niko, and Elisabeth Tinbergen. *Autistic Children: New Hope for a Cure*. London: George Allen & Unwin, 1983.

The Tinbergens apply the methods of ethology to autism. As a graduate student in anthropology, I cannot help but be excited by this merger between two of my major interests.

Contemporary Community Health Series

The Aging: A Guide to Public Policy
Bennett M. Rich and Martha Baum

Autistic Children: A Working Diary
Florence Milnes Kozak

Child Care Work with Emotionally Disturbed Children
Genevieve W. Foster et al.

Children in Jeopardy: A Study of Abused Minors and Their Families
Elizabeth Elmer

Clifford W. Beers: Advocate for the Insane
Norman Dain

Culture and Curing: Anthropological Perspectives on Traditional Medical Beliefs and Practices
Peter Morley and Roy Wallis, Editors

The Deepening Shade: Psychological Aspects of Life-Threatening Illness
Barbara M. Sourkes

The Doctor Tree: Developmental Stages in the Growth of Physicians
Ralph N. Zabarenko and Lucy M. Zabarenko

Fragile Families, Troubled Children: The Aftermath of Infant Trauma
Elizabeth Elmer

A Guide to Mental Health Services
Edward T. Heck, Angel G. Gomez, and George L. Adams

Handicap: A Study of Physically Handicapped Children and Their Families
Joan K. McMichael

Health Care in the European Community
Alan Maynard

Home and Hospital Psychiatric Treatment: An Interdisciplinary Experiment
Fred R. Fenton et al.

Literature and Medicine: An Annotated Bibliography
Joanne Trautmann and Carol Pollard

A Mad People's History of Madness
Dale Peterson, Editor

A Mind That Found Itself
Clifford W. Beers

The Psychiatric Halfway House: A Handbook of Theory and Practice
Richard D. Budson

Racism and Mental Health: Essays
Charles V. Willie, Bernard M. Kramer, and Bertram S. Brown, Editors

The Sociology of Physical Disability and Rehabilitation
Gary L. Albrecht, Editor

In cooperation with the Institute on Human Values in Medicine:

Medicine and Religion: Strategies of Care
Donald W. Shriver, Editor

Nourishing the Humanistic in Medicine: Interactions with the Social Sciences
William R. Rogers and David Barnard, Editors